YOUR PERSONAL
ASTROLOGY
PLANNER

SCORPIO
2008

YOUR PERSONAL

ASTROLOGY

PLANNER

SCORPIO
2008

RICK LEVINE **& JEFF** JAWER

STERLING

New York / London
www.sterlingpublishing.com

STERLING and the distinctive Sterling logo are registered
trademarks of Sterling Publishing Co., Inc.

Library of Congress Cataloging-in-Publication Data Available

2 4 6 8 10 9 7 5 3 1

Published by Sterling Publishing Co., Inc.
387 Park Avenue South, New York, NY 10016
© 2007 by Sterling Publishing Co., Inc.
Text © 2007 Rick Levine and Jeff Jawer
Distributed in Canada by Sterling Publishing
c/o Canadian Manda Group, 165 Dufferin Street
Toronto, Ontario, Canada M6K 3H6
Distributed in the United Kingdom by GMC Distribution Services
Castle Place, 166 High Street, Lewes, East Sussex, England BN7 1XU
Distributed in Australia by Capricorn Link (Australia) Pty. Ltd.
P.O. Box 704, Windsor, NSW 2756, Australia

Original book design: 3+Co., New York

Sterling ISBN-13: 978-1-4027-4851-6
ISBN-10: 1-4027-4851-5

For information about custom editions, special sales, premium and
corporate purchases, please contact Sterling Special Sales
Department at 800-805-5489 or specialsales@sterlingpub.com.

TABLE OF CONTENTS

THE PURPOSE OF THIS BOOK

The more you learn about yourself, the better able you are to wisely use the energies in your life. For more than 3,000 years, astrology has been the sharpest tool in the box for describing the human condition. Used by virtually every culture on the planet, astrology continues to serve as a link between individual lives and planetary cycles. We gain valuable insights into personal issues with a birth chart, and can plot the patterns of the year ahead in meaningful ways for individuals as well as groups. You share your sun sign with eight percent of humanity. Clearly, you're not all going to have the same day, even if the basic astrological cycles are the same. Your individual circumstances, the specific factors of your entire birth chart, and your own free will help you write your unique story.

The purpose of this book is to describe the energies of the Sun, Moon, and planets for the year ahead and help you create your future, rather than being a victim of it. We aim to facilitate your journey by showing you the turns ahead in the road of life and hopefully the best ways to navigate them.

YOU ARE THE STAR
OF YOUR LIFE

It is not our goal to simply predict events. Rather, we are reporting the planetary energies—the cosmic weather in which you are living—so that you understand these conditions and know how to use them most effectively.

The power, though, isn't in the stars, but in your mind, your heart, and the choices that you make every day. Regardless of how strongly you are buffeted by the winds of change or bored by stagnation, you have many ways to view any situation. Learning about the energies of the Sun, Moon, and planets will both sharpen and widen your perspective, thereby giving you additional choices.

The language of astrology is a gift of awareness, not a rigid set of rules. It works best when blended with common sense, intuition, and self-trust. This is your life, and no one knows how to live it as well as you. Take what you need from this book and leave the rest. Although the planets set the stage for the year ahead, you're the writer, director, and star of your life and you can play the part in whatever way you choose. *Your Personal Astrology Planner* uses information about your sun sign to give you a better understanding of how the planetary waves will wash upon your shore. We each navigate our lives through time, and each moment has unique qualities. Astrology gives us the ability to describe the constantly changing timescape. For example, if you know the trajectory and the speed of an approaching storm, you can choose to delay a leisurely afternoon sail on the bay, thus avoiding an unpleasant situation.

By reading this book, you can improve your ability to align with the cosmic weather, the larger patterns that affect you day to day. You can become more effective by aligning with the cosmos and cocreating the year ahead with a better understanding of the energies around you.

Astrology doesn't provide quick fixes to life's complex issues. It doesn't offer neatly packed black-and-white answers in a world filled with an infinite variety of shapes and colors. It can, however, give you a much clearer picture of the invisible forces influencing your life.

ENERGY & EVENTS

Two sailboats can face the same gale yet travel in opposite directions as a result of how the sails are positioned. Similarly, how you respond to the energy of a particular set of circumstances may be more responsible for your fate than the given situation itself. We delineate the energetic winds for your year ahead, but your attitude shapes the unfolding events, and your responses alter your destiny.

This book emphasizes the positive, not because all is good, but because astrology shows us ways to transform even the power of a storm into beneficial results. Empowerment comes from learning to see the invisible energy patterns that impact the visible landscape as you fill in the details of your story every day on this spinning planet, orbited by the Moon, lit by the Sun, and colored by the nuances of the planets.

You are a unique point in an infinite galaxy of unlimited possibilities, and the choices that you make have consequences. So use this book in a most magical way to consciously improve your life.

MOON CHARTS

2008 NEW MOONS

Each New Moon marks the beginning of a cycle. In general, this is the best time to plant seeds for future growth. Use the days preceeding the New Moon to finish old business prior to starting what comes next. The focused mind can be quite sharp during this phase. Harness the potential of the New Moon by stating your intentions—out loud or in writing—for the weeks ahead. Hold these goals in your mind; help them grow to fruition through conscious actions as the Moon gains light during the following two weeks. In the chart below, the dates and times refer to when the Moon and Sun align in each zodiac sign (see p16), initiating a new lunar cycle.

DATE	TIME	SIGN
January 8	6:37 AM EST	Capricorn
February 6	10:43 PM EST	Aquarius **(ECLIPSE)**
March 7	12:13 PM EST	Pisces
April 5	11:54 PM EDT	Aries
May 5	8:18 AM EDT	Taurus
June 3	3:22 PM EDT	Gemini
July 2	10:19 PM EDT	Cancer
August 1	6:12 AM EDT	Leo **(ECLIPSE)**
August 30	3:58 PM EDT	Virgo
September 29	4:12 AM EDT	Libra
October 28	7:14 PM EDT	Scorpio
November 27	11:54 AM EST	Sagittarius
December 27	7:22 AM EST	Capricorn

2008 FULL MOONS

The Full Moon reflects the light of the Sun as subjective feelings reflect the objective events of the day. Dreams seem bigger; moods feel stronger. The emotional waters run with deeper currents. This is the phase of culmination, a turning point in the energetic cycle. Now it's time to listen to the inner voices. Rather than starting new projects, the two weeks after the Full Moon are when we complete what we can and slow our outward expressions in anticipation of the next New Moon. In this chart, the dates and times refer to when the moon is opposite the sun in each zodiac sign, marking the emotional peak of each lunar cycle.

DATE	TIME	SIGN
January 22	8:35 AM EST	Leo
February 20	10:31 PM EST	Virgo **(ECLIPSE)**
March 21	2:40 PM EDT	Libra
April 20	6:25 AM EDT	Scorpio
May 19	10:11 PM EDT	Scorpio
June 18	1:30 PM EDT	Sagittarius
July 18	3:58 AM EDT	Capricorn
August 16	5:16 PM EDT	Aquarius **(ECLIPSE)**
September 15	5:13 AM EDT	Pisces
October 14	4:01 PM EDT	Aries
November 13	1:16 AM EST	Taurus
December 12	11:37 AM EST	Gemini

ASTROLOGY, YOU & THE WORLD

WELCOME TO YOUR SUN SIGN

The Sun, Moon, and Earth and all the planets lie within a plane called the **ecliptic** and move through a narrow band of stars made up by 12 constellations called the **zodiac**. The Earth revolves around the Sun once a year, but from our point of view, it appears that the Sun moves through each sign of the zodiac for one month. There are 12 months and astrologically there are 12 signs. The astrological months, however, do not match our calendar, and start between the 19th and 23rd of each month. Everyone is born to an astrological month, like being born in a room with a particular perspective of the world. Knowing your sun sign provides useful information about your personality and your future, but for a more detailed astrological analysis, a full birth chart calculation based on your precise date, time, and place of birth is necessary. Get your complete birth chart online at:

http://www.tarot.com/astrology/astroprofile

This book is about your zodiac sign. Your Sun is in the intensely emotional water sign of Scorpio. Whether you're the kind of Scorpio who keeps feelings secret or who shares them with the world, power and intuition reside at the depths of your being. You can draw on your instincts to overcome almost any obstacle and to heal, motivate, and manage others. Whatever it is, Scorpio, you almost never do anything halfway. It's all or nothing for you.

THE PLANETS

We refer to the Sun and Moon as planets. Don't worry; we do know about modern astronomy. Although the Sun is really a star and the Moon is a satellite, they are called planets for astrological purposes. The astrological planets are the Sun, the Moon, Mercury, Venus, Mars, Jupiter, Saturn, Chiron, Uranus, Neptune, and Pluto.

Your sun sign is the most obvious astrological placement, for the Sun returns to the same sign every year. But at the same time, the Moon is orbiting the Earth, changing signs every two and a third days. Mercury, Venus, and Mars each move through a sign in a few weeks to a few months.

Jupiter spends a whole year in a sign—and Pluto visits a sign for up to 30 years! The ever-changing positions of the planets alter the energetic terrain through which we travel. The planets are symbols; each has a particular range of meanings. For example, Venus is the goddess of love, but it really symbolizes beauty in a spectrum of experiences. Venus can represent romantic love, sensuality, the arts, or good food. It activates anything that we value, including personal possessions and even money. To our ancestors, the planets actually animated life on Earth. In this way of thinking, every beautiful flower contains the essence of Venus.

Each sign has a natural affinity to an individual planet, and as this planet moves through the sky, it sends messages of particular interest to people born under that sign. Mars is your traditional key or ruling planet, and Pluto is the modern ruler of your sign. Mars triggers action and provokes passion or anger. Pluto leads you to the very bottom of whatever is of concern to you. It strips away the unessential so that you can concentrate on the heart of the matter. Planets can be described by many different words, for the mythology of each is a rich tapestry. In this book we use a variety of words when talking about each planet in order to convey the most applicable meaning. The table below describes a few keywords for each planet, including the Sun and Moon.

PLANET	SYMBOL	KEYWORDS
Sun	☉	Consciousness, Will, Vitality
Moon	☽	Subconscious, Emotions, Habits
Mercury	☿	Communication, Thoughts, Transportation
Venus	♀	Desire, Love, Money, Values
Mars	♂	Action, Physical Energy, Drive
Jupiter	♃	Expansion, Growth, Optimism
Saturn	♄	Contraction, Maturity, Responsibility
Chiron	⚷	Healing, Pain, Subversion
Uranus	♅	Awakening, Unpredictable, Inventive
Neptune	♆	Imagination, Spirituality, Confusion
Pluto	♇	Passion, Intensity, Regeneration

HOUSES

Just as planets move through the signs of the zodiac, they also move through the houses in an individual chart. The 12 houses correspond to the 12 signs, but are individualized, based upon your sign. In this book we use Solar Houses, which place your sun sign in your 1st House. Therefore, when a planet enters a new sign it also enters a new house. If you know your exact time of birth, the rising sign determines the 1st House. You can learn your rising sign by entering your birth date at:

http://www.tarot.com/astrology/astroprofile

HOUSE	SIGN	KEYWORDS
1st House	Aries	Self, Appearance, Personality
2nd House	Taurus	Possessions, Values, Self-Worth
3rd House	Gemini	Communication, Siblings, Short Trips
4th House	Cancer	Home, Family, Roots
5th House	Leo	Love, Romance, Children, Play
6th House	Virgo	Work, Health, Daily Routines
7th House	Libra	Marriage, Relationships, Business Partners
8th House	Scorpio	Intimacy, Transformation, Shared Resources
9th House	Sagittarius	Travel, Higher Education, Philosophy
10th House	Capricorn	Career, Community, Ambition
11th House	Aquarius	Groups and Friends, Associations, Social Ideals
12th House	Pisces	Imagination, Spirituality, Secret Activities

ASPECTS

As the planets move through the sky in their various cycles, they form ever-changing angles with one another. Certain angles create significant geometric shapes. So, when two planets are 90 degrees apart, they conform to a square; 60 degrees of separation conforms to a sextile, or six-pointed star. Planets create **aspects** when they're at these special angles. Aspects explain how the individual symbolism of pairs of planets combine into an energetic pattern.

ASPECT	DEGREES	KEYWORDS
Conjunction	0	Compression, Blending, Focus
Opposition	180	Tension, Awareness, Balance
Trine	120	Harmony, Free-Flowing, Ease
Square	90	Resistance, Stress, Dynamic Conflict
Quintile	72	Creativity, Metaphysical, Magic
Sextile	60	Support, Intelligent, Activating
Quincunx	150	Irritation, Annoyance, Adjustment

2008 GENERAL FORECAST:
THE INDIVIDUAL AND THE COLLECTIVE

Astrology works for individuals, groups, and even humanity as a whole. You will have your own story in 2008, but it will unfold among 6.7 billion other tales of human experience. We are each unique, yet our lives touch one another; our destinies are woven together by weather and war, by economy, science, politics, religion, and all the other threads of life on this planet. We make personal choices every day, yet there are great events beyond the control of any one individual. When the power goes out in a neighborhood, it affects everyone, yet individual astrology patterns will describe the personal response of each person.

We are living at a time when the tools of self-awareness fill bookshelves, Web sites, and broadcasts, and we benefit greatly from them. Yet despite all this wisdom, conflicts among groups cause enormous suffering. Understanding personal issues is a powerful means for increasing happiness, but knowledge of our collective issues is equally important for our well-being. This forecast of the major trends and planetary patterns for 2008 provides a

framework for understanding the potentials and
challenges we face together, so that we can advance
with tolerance and respect as a community and ful-
fill our potentials as individuals.

The astrological events used for this forecast are
the transits of major planets Jupiter and Saturn,
the retrograde cycles of Mercury, and the eclipses
of the Sun and the Moon.

A NOTE ABOUT THE DATES IN THIS BOOK

All events are based upon the Eastern Time Zone of the United
States. Because of local time differences, an event occurring
just minutes after midnight in the East will actually happen
the prior day in the rest of the country. Although the key dates
are the exact dates of any particular alignment, some of you
are so ready for certain things to happen that you can react to
a transit a day or two before it is exact. And sometimes you
could be so entrenched in habits or unwilling to change that
you may not notice the effects right away. Allow extra time
around each key date to feel the impact of any event.

JUPITER IN CAPRICORN
MATERIALIZING SUCCESS
December 18, 2007–January 5, 2009

Optimistic Jupiter is ready to climb a mountain this year.
Instead of simply heading off on an adventure, the

planet of expansion's passage through industrious Capricorn is a time to set goals, plan a course of action, and reach the summit of success. Jolly Jupiter is usually happy exploring the world, seeking new experiences, and expanding the mind. But Saturn-ruled Capricorn puts the giant planet in a productive mood where the name of the game is getting results. Opportunities come for those who do their homework and demonstrate the patience and commitment to prove their worthiness. There's less room for sloppiness for those who want chance to turn in their favor. Good luck is earned only by solid effort this year.

Jupiter in Capricorn is a time to turn beliefs into reality. Idealistic philosophies lose their meaning unless practice brings them down to earth. The enormous planet loves the biggest ideas, but Capricorn's practicality will test them against the weight of experience. The dark side of Jupiter's presence here is materialism that values worldly achievement more than spiritual awakening. Instead of living up to standards that may be difficult to reach, it will be tempting to lower those standards or just do away with them entirely.

Hope for a balanced approach to ambition occurs with positive trines between Jupiter and Saturn in January, September, and November. These healthy alignments between the planets of expansion and contraction bring the wisdom of self-restraint and a willingness to earn one's rewards honestly. Those who play by the rules should get what they deserve, while those who cut corners are likely to slide right off the track and slip farther from their aspirations. The Jupiter-Saturn trine in earth signs adds conscientiousness and a capacity to put in the time necessary to attain one's goals.

Positive 60-degree sextiles between Jupiter and inventive Uranus in late March, May, and November supply a plethora of fresh ideas that help us avoid repeating old mistakes. The pragmatism of Jupiter and Saturn in earth signs has a conservative side that would normally resist untested concepts. But Uranus's aspects with Jupiter weave intuition into the year's fabric to brighten it with originality. Jupiter's friendly relation-ships with the planets of the old tried and true (Saturn) and new and untested (Uranus) combines the best of the past and the future.

SATURN IN VIRGO
MANAGING THE DETAILS
September 2, 2007–October 29, 2009

Saturn, the planet of boundaries and limitations, takes twenty-nine years to orbit the Sun and pass through all twelve signs of the zodiac. It demands serious respon-sibility, shows the work needed to overcome obstacles, and teaches us how to build new structures in our lives. Saturn thrives on patience and commitment, rewarding well-planned and persistent effort but punishing sloppi-ness with delay, disappointment, and failure.

Saturn's passage through detail-oriented Virgo is a time to perfect skills, cut waste, and develop healthier habits. Saturn and Virgo are both pragmatic, which makes them an excellent pair for improving the quality of material life. Organizational upgrades and maintenance projects increase efficiency for individuals and organizations. Education and training become more valuable due to the increasing demand for highly specialized skills. Carelessness grows more costly, because minor errors can escalate into major problems. Systems break down easily, requiring closer attention than usual. Bodies can be more susceptible to illnesses caused by impure food or water, making this an ideal time to improve your diet. Environmental issues grow in importance as we approach a critical point in the relationship between humanity and planet Earth. Fortunately, Saturn in exacting Virgo is excellent for cleaning up unhealthy toxins produced by old technologies and in leading the way to develop new ecologically friendly systems for the future.

Saturn in Virgo highlights flaws and makes it easier to be critical of oneself and others. Yet its true purpose is to solve problems, not simply complain about them. Recognizing our weaknesses can sometimes be a source of despair, but the functional combination of Saturn's commitment and Virgo's analytical skills gives hope that effective change is well within our grasp. Small steps in a positive direction can slowly build up to a tidal wave of improvement wherever you place your attention this year.

MERCURY RETROGRADES
January 28–February 18 in Aquarius / May 26–June 19 in Gemini / September 23–October 15 in Libra

All true planets appear to move retrograde from time to time as a result of viewing them from the moving platform of Earth. The most significant retrograde periods are those of Mercury, the communication planet. Occurring three times a year for roughly three weeks at a time, these are periods when difficulties with details, travel, information flow, and technical matters are likely.

Although Mercury's retrograde phase has received a fair amount of bad press, it isn't necessarily a negative cycle. Because personal and commercial interactions are emphasized, you can actually accomplish more than usual, especially if you stay focused on what needs to be done rather than initiating new projects. But you may feel as if you're treading water—or worse yet, being carried backward in an undertow of unfinished business. Worry less about making progress than about the quality of your work. Pay extra attention to your communication exchanges. Avoiding misunderstandings is the ideal way to preemptively deal with unnecessary complications. Retrograde Mercury is best used to tie up loose ends as you review, redo, reconsider, and, in general, revisit the past.

This year, the three retrogrades are in intellectual air signs (Aquarius, Gemini, and Libra), which can be very useful for analysis and remedial studies that help you reevaluate what you already know so you can take your learning to the next step. Mercury has a natural affinity for the air signs, so you are empowered by your mental prowess during these times. But however intelligent you feel, don't become so enamored with the workings of your mind that you forget about the practical aspects of your body and the emotional needs of your heart.

ECLIPSES
Solar: February 6 and August 1
Lunar: February 20 and August 16

Solar and Lunar Eclipses are special New and Full Moons that indicate meaningful changes for individuals and groups. They are powerful markers of events whose influences can appear up to three months in advance and last up to six months afterward.

February 6, Solar Eclipse in Aquarius: Community Concerns A revolutionary point of view can put an end to old fantasies and give birth to new dreams as mental Mercury and idealistic Neptune join the Sun and Moon during this eclipse. Aquarius allows a wide-spectrum view in which we can see our individual lives within the larger context of teams, groups, and community. Chiron, the Wounded Healer, also joins the eclipse point, which can increase compassion globally, give birth to new social organizations, and stir more interest in charitable activities. Charismatic leaders may emerge with fresh ideas for reinvigorating society. But it could be difficult to determine which are capable of bringing about real change and which are simply masters of illusion.

February 20, Lunar Eclipse in Virgo: Fix What's Broken
This total eclipse of the Moon in critical Virgo reveals flaws in current systems, regardless of how much effort was put into building them. Serious Saturn conjunct the Moon reflects the hard work invested in the physical and emotional structures that are starting to fail now. A Lunar Eclipse is about letting go of the past, but both the Moon and Saturn are resistant to change. Virgo's analytical abilities permit us to justify these outmoded patterns with reason and practicality. But the Pisces Sun in opposition shows that the creative path of faith and imagination will take us farther than roads of duty, obligation, and habit. When daily details drain the joy out of life, it's clear that change is necessary. Yet we may feel the need to choose between a reality that's not fully satisfying and a dream that we fear will never come true. Fortunately, evolutionary Pluto forms a creative 120-degree trine with the eclipse that eliminates nonessential tasks to free up time and energy for more meaningful activities.

August 1, Solar Eclipse in Leo: Creativity Shines
Eclipses of the Sun are often associated with the fall of leaders. This one in the Sun's own sign of Leo is visible through central Russia and China, where changes at the top are most likely to occur. On a personal level, Solar

Eclipses are reminders to tame the ego and to balance will with humility. At its best, Leo is a sign of creative expression and generosity, but at its worst it represents a petulant, demanding child. Oppositions to this Sun-Moon conjunction from Neptune and Chiron add vulnerability and engender the kind of insecurity that may provoke immature behavior. Expect drama, but don't allow it to take over. Instead of giving in to the demands of others or to your own fears, step back and permit the storm to pass. This eclipse can bring healing through self-acceptance and recognition that even the biggest stories are only chapters in the book of life.

August 16, Lunar Eclipse in Aquarius: Make New Friends
This partial Lunar Eclipse is joined with nebulous Neptune, which could bring floods and fraud into the headlines. Otherwise honorable organizations may be touched by scandal or exposed as severely underfunded. Individually, this eclipse is excellent for letting go of beliefs that don't correspond with your current reality. Outdated ideals or dreams may need to be discarded, which can be painful, but awakening to today's truth brings a breath of fresh air that clears clutter from the mind. Cooperation is the key with Aquarius, so recognizing where friends and allies are more hindrance than help is important.

Remember that all of these astrological events are part of the general cosmic weather for the year, but will affect us each differently based upon our individual astrological signs.

2008
HOROSCOPE

SCORPIO

OCTOBER 23–NOVEMBER 21

OVERVIEW OF THE YEAR

A big year lies ahead of you, complete with a few surprises that can complicate your life, yet fortunately you have the tools to integrate change with great ease. Optimistic Jupiter, realistic Saturn, and exciting Uranus create a major theme as you are ready to see opportunities through a practical filter, enabling you to steadily move toward your desired goals. Together, Jupiter and Saturn form a repeating pattern of harmonious trines—exact on January 21, September 8, and November 28—that balances your drive to succeed with the continued focus you need to reach your goals. What makes the Jupiter-Saturn trine so significant for you is that your sign, Scorpio, is safely nestled between these cosmic regulators, with confident Jupiter encouraging you to **expand your thinking to grow beyond your present level of awareness,** while practical Saturn simultaneously concentrates your energy inward so you don't scatter valuable resources. Saturn in your 11th House of Friends and Wishes requires you to **work cooperatively rather than venturing out on**

your own. You may not have the patience for the frivolous activities of others, yet being part of a team can help you be much more productive. Additionally, Saturn expects more from you than just meeting your day-to-day obligations; it expects you to honor your hopes and distant dreams.

This is a transitional year for you, beginning with an intense standoff between your two key planets, fiery Mars and domineering Pluto. As a Scorpio, you are particularly sensitive to the movements of Pluto. Your life was transformed when Pluto was in Scorpio between 1983 and 1995. Then, as Pluto moved through opinionated Sagittarius, you reexamined your core beliefs, discarding ideas, values, and possessions that no longer served you well. On January 25, this tiny concentrated bundle of planetary intensity leaves Sagittarius to enter hardworking Capricorn in your 3rd House of Communication. There it will force you to reevaluate the validity of your intellectual foundations.

A Jupiter-Uranus sextile—exact on March 28, May 21, and November 12—creates a positive environment for you to communicate more spontaneously, especially in matters of love or with children. **Tensions increase through the autumn** as restrictive Saturn engages in a cosmic tug-of-war with erratic Uranus—exact on November 4—in yet another long-term cycle that strongly influences your life through 2010. The viability of previous commitments is set against your need for individual self-expression, and although Jupiter blesses you with buoyant optimism through most of November, Mars's square to Saturn and Uranus on December 12–15 can drive your frustration to the surface, provoking you to take radical action to put your life back on track. All in all, **this is a year for you to make great strides forward in accomplishing your goals as long as you don't ride roughshod over the feelings of people around you.** With the year-long Mars-Pluto theme that is exact on January 2, March 7, August 17, and December 28, it's crucial to express your feelings constructively and calmly, instead of engaging someone you love in an unnecessary battle for dominance or even survival.

CALM BEFORE THE STORM

The cool Virgo Full Moon Eclipse on February 20 activates your love houses, yet its close proximity to serious Saturn throws obstacles in your path to pleasure. Manage these issues wisely and you can solidify a significant relationship. Generous Jupiter, the traditional ruler of your 5th House of Love, brings steady growth to romance as it moves through cautious Capricorn all year. Its trine to somber Saturn can quiet your excitement, which could be a dilemma since you are naturally intense. But it may also be a relief, for you have likely grown weary of romantic dramas due to unstable Uranus's extended journey through your 5th House, which began in 2003. Fulfilling commitments is important, but you may not be able hold back your irrepressible need for more independence as Saturn moves toward its life-changing opposition with Uranus—exact on November 4.

TEAM PLAYER

It's important to work with others rather than alone as career-minded Saturn moves through your 11th House of Teamwork. Although you may be naturally inclined to remain separate from the group, discipline involving ongoing interactions with your associates can keep you moving along the right track and improve your chances for success. The steadying Jupiter-Saturn trine strengthens the ideas upon which you build your career path, but eclipses also play an important role in your success this year. In particular, the dramatic Leo Solar Eclipse on August 1 falls in your 10th House of Public Status, and its proximity to mental Mercury suggests the necessity for bold communication. Nevertheless, be sure to discuss your plans with others before making major decisions on your own.

NO FREE LUNCH

Beneficent Jupiter, the ruler of your 2nd House of Money, is somewhat restrained this year as it moves through pragmatic Capricorn and is further limited by ongoing aspects with frugal Saturn. At first glance, this might sound like bad news—but it does indicate steady financial growth as long as you don't make any foolish moves. Avoid temptations to invest impulsively; if something appears too good to be true, it probably is, especially when overconfident Jupiter sextiles unreliable Uranus around March 28, May 21, and November 12. Keeping a tight rein on unnecessary expenditures during these times can really pay off as you increase your bank account with your hard work and smart long-term planning throughout the year.

LET'S GET PHYSICAL

Physical exercise is more important this year than ever before, regardless of your age and previous level of activity. The year begins and ends with energetic Mars, the ruler of your 6th House of Health, contacting transformational Pluto, making it critical to channel your overly intense feelings into action. If you work out regularly, it may be time to push yourself to the next level. On the other hand, if you don't have a daily regimen, join a gym, enroll in a yoga class, or start taking regular walks. The positive impact this will have on your health cannot be overstated. What's most important now is to realize that you have a chance to renew and regenerate, but it will take real commitment on your part, along with the necessary self-discipline to stick to your new routine.

SAFE HAVEN

Mercury's entry into your 4th House of Home and Family on January 7 can flood your mind with ideas for bringing more excitement and innovation into your personal life. Venus enters quirky Aquarius in your 4th House on February 17—staying there through March 12—indicating your potential for sharing good times with unconventional friends in the privacy of your own place. But it is dreamy Neptune in your 4th House all year that continues to remind you that your home is a place to retreat from the noise of the outer world. Here you can entertain the infinite possibilities of your imagination.

REVISIT YOUR PAST

Rather than expending excess energy on vacations this year, you are more likely to travel with a specific purpose in mind as Jupiter, the planet of distant horizons, harmoniously trines practical Saturn. Mars enters your 9th House of Travel on March 4, remaining there through May 9, firing you with desire to get up and go. However, its movement through self-protective Cancer suggests that you may return to a favorite spot from the past or revisit a childhood home instead of heading off to someplace new. Although it may not be your first inclination, don't be afraid to follow a whim and go somewhere different for a change.

INNER GROWTH, OUTER WORK

Your physical and metaphysical growth are exceptionally intertwined this year as Pluto, the planet of metamorphosis, pushes you into new territory while facing strong resistance from repeated tense aspects with "action oriented" Mars. Your challenge is to express yourself creatively rather than avoiding the stress. Imaginative Neptune's involvement in three out of four eclipses this year suggests the important role spiritual practice plays in unlocking the doors of potential. You can facilitate transformation by working on subtle inner planes while improving your mastery over physical limitations. It's more crucial than ever to blend your dream work, meditation, and the power of positive thought with all your actions in the outer world.

RICK & JEFF'S TIP FOR THE YEAR
Shorten Your To-Do List

Although you are eager to test the ground in a
new world, temper your optimism with reason
and caution. Even if you feel a great sense of
urgency about making sweeping changes to
the fundamental underpinnings of your life,
remember that you don't have to make them
all at once. In fact, shifting several routines
too quickly can create turmoil that is more
detrimental than helpful. Instead of scattering
your energies, prioritize your needs and initiate
only a few changes that will have lasting impact.
Remember, what you set into motion now
may take many years to reach fruition.

JANUARY

DELAYED SATISFACTION

The opening days of January pack a punch of adrenaline, but it's misleading, for your movement may be stymied throughout the month. Your two key planets, energetic Mars and fixed Pluto, form a tense opposition on **January 2**, bringing resistance from a mighty opponent. This sets the stage for power struggles through **March 7**, when Mars again faces Pluto. Mars is retrograde until **January 30**, potentially turning your frustration into anger while forcing you to revisit ground covered last September. You cannot escape the pressure that comes from interacting with others now: Mars in your 8th House of Shared Resources emphasizes the partnerships you must maintain to enrich your life. Optimistic Jupiter harmonizes with realistic Saturn on **January 21**, the first of three such trines that repeat on **September 8 and November 21**. Stability is your key to success, making January a prime time to create a long-term strategy for achieving your goals by year's end. The earthy Capricorn New Moon on **January 8** is one more reminder of the importance of cautious practicality over reckless abandon.

As if there weren't enough planetary pressure preventing your professional progress, intelligent Mercury crawls along slowly until it turns retrograde on **January 28**, disrupting your thoughts and plans. The dramatic Leo Full Moon on **January 22** brings out your extreme nature, especially as sensual Venus pushes toward a conjunction with potent Pluto on **January 24**, stirring your passions and driving you to experience emotional heights. However, the ecstatic feelings may rebound, pushing you into darker places that you also wish to explore. You may be disappointed if someone is not yet willing to go there to share in the discovery.

KEEP IN MIND THIS MONTH

Your strong urge to merge with someone special takes longer to happen than you wish. Handle your frustration with a long-term perspective and not by seeking short-term gratification.

KEY DATES

SUPER NOVA DAY

★ **JANUARY 2**
fight to the finish

You may be feeling suspicious as self-directed Mars—now retrograde and less effective than normal—meets tyrannical Pluto in a cosmic standoff. If someone is undermining your efforts, it might seem as if your reputation or even your survival is at stake. Whether or not this is true, it's time to step up and confront the issues, for if you try to keep everything light and breezy you'll only make matters worse. Look back to **September 21, 2007**, for the possible origin of this conflict. If you respond out of fear, you'll only fuel the drama. Adding a bit of self-control to your passion can be an unbeatable combination, especially since full resolution may not occur until **March 7**, when Mars direct repeats the aspect for the third and final time.

★ **JANUARY 9–13**
practical magic
These days are blessed by an unusual pattern:
Mental Mercury, physical Mars, and wise
Saturn mark three points of a magical five-
pointed star. Mars biquintiles Mercury on
January 9 and quintiles Saturn on **January 13**,
revealing the charisma and creativity bubbling
up from the deep pool of your imagination.
Even the most original thoughts can now be
applied in the real world, though you must
take the initiative to express the best ones.
Still, be careful—sweet Venus squares wild
Uranus on **January 12**, attracting you toward
love and freedom simultaneously. Don't set
aside your ambitious aspirations to act on
every unconventional desire that runs through
your mind or you'll find more trouble than you
can manage.

★ **JANUARY 19–21**
build a bridge
Relationship discord mounts as Venus and
Mars, the cosmic lovers, pull you in opposite
directions on **January 19**. Anxiety can build

walls between you and your partner, but the tension can be handled if you are willing to listen to what someone else wants. Remaining open to a new perspective gives you a way to process the stress—either emotionally or physically—and create the romantic magic you were seeking all along. Fortunately, you receive additional support from the stabilizing Jupiter-Saturn trine on **January 21**, strengthening your commitment to love.

★ **JANUARY 22–24**
a walk on the dark side
The fixed Leo Full Moon on **January 22** falls in your 10th House of Public Status, so everyone will likely know exactly how you are feeling. But a conjunction between mental Mercury and foggy Neptune suggests that you may not be able to clearly explain your mood. Beautiful Venus joins dark Pluto on **January 24**, driving your intense desires out from the shadows of your mind. Although your stress levels may be high, this is not a permanent condition. Facing your fears is not as dangerous as suppressing them in the long run.

FEBRUARY

TIGHTEN YOUR PLANS

You may feel somewhat scattered this month as self-directed Mars moves ahead in versatile Gemini. And although you are eager to push your life forward on a variety of fronts, mental Mercury is retrograde until **February 18**, tying your thoughts to the past. Nevertheless, you may be quite optimistic as the month unfolds, for lovely Venus joins beneficial Jupiter on **February 1** in earthy Capricorn, where they tempt you with the sweet fruits of pleasure. You can have what you want as long as you take your commitments seriously and play by the rules. Still, you may be caught off guard as the quirky Aquarius New Moon Eclipse on **February 6** in your 4th House of Roots changes your mind about what security means to you. You may be suddenly inspired to shake up stagnant energy at home—and even if you do this with the best of intentions, you could stir up a hornet's nest of fear. Painful memories of old family conflicts can burst into consciousness, possibly causing you to overreact and aggravate the situation.

You are nudged into new territory when Venus enters progressive Aquarius on **February 17**,

Mercury turns direct on **February 18**, and the Sun enters compassionate Pisces on **February 19**. These transitional days prepare you for the focused thinking you must do during the analytical Virgo Full Moon Eclipse on **February 20**. The Sun's annual opposition to responsible Saturn on **February 24** can illuminate the shortcomings of a current strategy by revealing obstacles to your development. Don't just give up: Accept whatever difficult news you hear with grace while promising yourself to do whatever is necessary to reach your destination.

KEEP IN MIND THIS MONTH

Instead of racing off in several directions without a cohesive strategy, reevaluate your plans to take into consideration the unexpected information you receive throughout the month.

KEY DATES

★ **FEBRUARY 1–2**
inner voices
Beautiful Venus's conjunction with optimistic
Jupiter on **February 1** encourages you to gloss
over the more serious problems of the day
because your life appears to be looking up. This
can be quite healing, allowing you to take a
mental holiday away from the issues that have
been troubling you. But retrograde Mercury's
conjunction with imaginary Neptune on
February 2 can confuse boundaries, stimulate
fantasies, and make it difficult to sustain your
confidence. Put off big decisions for now, but
pay close attention to your dreams for the
guidance you need.

SUPER NOVA DAYS

★ **FEBRUARY 6–7**
change the rules
An emotionally revealing Aquarius Solar Eclipse
on **February 6** in your 4th House of Home
and Family can bring a shock, but you will be
better off once you are armed with the truth.

53

Fortunately, harmonious trines to "action hero" Mars in clever Gemini help you dance through a recurring family drama. Additionally, a magical quintile between Mars and authoritative Saturn on **February 7** issues you a needed reality check. Although you could bump into walls of restraint, they won't stop your progress. The transformative nature of the quintile gives you the tools to change the rules instead of fighting them.

★ **FEBRUARY 13–14**
integrity counts
Your desires may remain unfulfilled with sexy Venus quincunxing aggressive Mars on **February 13** in an irritating emotional standoff as you attempt to gain control of an unmanageable situation. You are awkwardly torn as you search for an elusive balance between withholding your feelings and saying too much. Luckily, the Sun harmoniously trines Mars on **February 14**, so others will appreciate your directness if you combine it with honesty. Even if you are sure that you were right all along, an overt gesture of reconciliation is worth more than a thousand well-intended thoughts.

★ **FEBRUARY 20**
choose logic
The intuitive Pisces Sun lights up your life,
yet the practical Virgo Full Moon Eclipse on
February 20 sets your pragmatic logic against
the whims of your heart. The Moon is conjunct
austere Saturn in your 11th House of Dreams
and Wishes, adding an inarguable sense of
reality to your thinking. Trust these thoughts,
for your sound judgment can now show you
the best path forward.

★ **FEBRUARY 24**
rise to the challenge
Although you want to go out and play, the
Sun's tense opposition to Saturn may require
you to wait. Even if you can't join in the fun,
this temporary barrier can provide just the
right amount of resistance to force you to concentrate. Don't give others a reason to judge
you negatively; just focus on taking one small
step at a time in order to reach your goal.

MARCH

CRAZY LOVE

You have had time enough to prepare; now you need to swing into action. Mars's entry into emotionally protective Cancer on **March 4** in your 9th House of Big Ideas indicates the close connection between your feelings and your behavior this month. Avoid the temptation of isolating yourself behind a hard outer shell. Taking a calculated risk can catalyze your life and set your long-term plans into motion. But your will may be pitted against someone else's as Mars opposes domineering Pluto on **March 7**. Happily, romantic Venus enters Pisces in your 5th House of Fun and Games on **March 12**, followed by Mercury on **March 14**, emphasizing the importance of expressing yourself spontaneously. Rediscovering the joy of your inner child can turn this month into quite a memorable one. But it's not all laughter, for both Venus and Mercury oppose restrictive Saturn on **March 15–17**. Acknowledging your responsibilities, realizing your shortcomings, or just coming to grips with the stark reality of a current situation can be depressing at first, but facing the truth can surprisingly also set you free.

You are highly motivated to overcome any feelings of low self-esteem as Venus and Mercury move on to support assertive Mars on **March 16–18**. The Sun's rejuvenating entry into enthusiastic Aries on **March 20** marks the Spring Equinox, illuminating your 6th House of Health and Work. You are excited about tackling what's next, but the indecisive Libra Full Moon on **March 21** can temporarily overwhelm you with conflicting feelings about your relationships. Mercury and Venus, still traveling through psychic Pisces together, join explosive Uranus on **March 27–28**, blasting you with sudden awareness and leading you toward a truth you have been avoiding.

KEEP IN MIND THIS MONTH

Passive acquiescence is no more an option than telling everyone exactly what you think. Soften your extremes by choosing a path of moderation and kindness.

KEY DATES

SUPER NOVA DAYS

★ **MARCH 7–8**
the high price of self-expression

Even the smallest disagreements can escalate into serious struggles as touchy Mars opposes potent Pluto on **March 7**, firing up your passions so strongly they cannot be suppressed. You are ready to play for keeps if a powerful opponent attempts to undermine your efforts. It may be difficult to keep everything in perspective, for you are easily provoked right now as the imaginative Pisces New Moon joins reckless Uranus in your 5th House of Self-Expression. When the Sun joins Uranus on **March 8**, a flash of inspiration suddenly shifts your perspective. Although it still may be a challenge to let go of your fears, at least a more humorous approach can move the energy into a healthier place.

★ **MARCH 14–18**
healthy outlets

You may feel a bit defeated as friendly Venus and sweet-talking Mercury stand opposed to stern Saturn on **March 15 and March 17**. You needn't, though, for a readjustment to your plans may leave you in better shape than before. Assistance arrives from the supportive sextile between energetic Mars and Saturn on **March 14**, giving you the organizational skills you need, along with sufficient fortitude to meet any resistance. Additionally, Venus's and Mercury's trines to Mars on **March 16 and March 18** can smooth over the rough spots. Try balancing your responsibilities with playful activities involving children. Expressing your own inner poet through creative or romantic pursuits can also reduce the current pressure.

★ **MARCH 21**
conflict management
This can be an intense day as the combative Aries Sun and the diplomatic Libra Full Moon cross paths with passionate Pluto, putting you at odds with someone in your immediate environment. If it feels like others are working against you, give them good reason to support you instead of fanning the fires of conflict. It may be better to get physical and sweat it out

as the Moon wanes over the next few days. Venting your frustration now, Scorpio, will only make matters worse.

★ **MARCH 28–30**
magnetic appeal
Your amorous attractions break out of constraints on **March 28** as Venus conjoins radical Uranus in your 5th House of Romance. Together they form a supportive sextile with optimistic Jupiter, filling you with an outrageous confidence that emboldens you to extend your reach and take advantage of an unusual opportunity. But the Sun's dynamic square to manipulative Mars on **March 30** produces disagreements over something that won't really matter in the long run. Find constructive ways to express your negativity so you can end the month on a positive note rather than wasting energy in needless conflict.

APRIL

BATTEN DOWN THE HATCHES

April brings an odd mixture of practical solutions
to complex problems that can stabilize your life.
At times, however, you may have so much enthusiasm about the potential of what lies ahead that
you can get yourself in trouble by taking on more
than you can handle. The excitement begins as
mental Mercury talks its way into eager Aries on
April 2, followed by stylish Venus on **April 6**. Both
of these planets immediately encounter dynamic
squares to potent Pluto, demanding that you justify your new ideas and desires before taking them
any further. The Aries New Moon on **April 5** in
your 6th House of Health and Daily Routines
dares you to start the spring cleaning that's been
on your mind, whether it involves chores around
the house and office or altering your lifestyle with
healthy new habits in order to rejuvenate your body.

Throughout the first part of the month, you are
called upon to resolve your stress by taking the
initiative anywhere you can, often with small steps
that can bring about larger changes over time.
But as the Moon waxes full, Mercury enters
dependable Taurus on **April 17**, followed by the

Sun on **April 19**, creating Grand Earth Trines with constructive Saturn and powerful Pluto. The Scorpio Full Moon on **April 20** can be an intense confirmation of the path you have chosen. Common sense combined with cautious optimism allows you to capture the importance of this moment in a cohesive plan that can solidify a significant relationship. Things seem to be going your way, yet a high-energy trine between Mars and surprising Uranus sets the stage for you to act impulsively due to unrealistic overconfidence influenced by Mars's opposition to fearless Jupiter on **April 24**.

KEEP IN MIND THIS MONTH

These are tricky times. You may need to temper your desire for immediate satisfaction by keeping your eyes on the distant prize.

KEY DATES

★ **APRIL 3–6**
boiling point
The impatient Aries New Moon on **April 5** urges
you to get your feelings out into the open;
however, you may feel forced to say something
you would prefer keeping private. Your mind—
influenced by quicksilver Mercury in speedy
Aries squaring compulsive Pluto on **April 3**—
is thinking faster than your heart can process
the data. Attractive Venus squares Pluto on
April 6, drawing you further into a complex
web of feelings. You must find ways to bring
positive change into your life or the volcanic
emotional pressures could erupt and complicate
an already tense situation.

★ **APRIL 10**
out of proportion
The Sun squares expansive Jupiter, tempting
you with opportunities that look too good to
be true. Your optimism can fuel your actions,
helping you accomplish more than usual as
long as you don't take on too much. Be careful,

for communicator Mercury squares pushy
Mars, triggering you to say more than you
intend, possibly stirring an argument driven
by ego and not by necessity. Channel your
aggression into cooperative efforts instead
of divisive ones.

SUPER NOVA DAYS

★ **APRIL 18–21**
conscious intent
You could lose a few days of harmony if you let
yourself get overwhelmed by the passionate
Scorpio Full Moon on **April 20**. Fortunately, the
intensity is ameliorated by trines from logical
Mercury and the Sun to heavyweights Saturn
and Pluto. Mercury completes a Grand Earth
Trine on **April 18**, concentrating your intentions
on meaningful activities. The Sun illuminates
this same grand trine on **April 20–21**, adding
the strength of conviction to your words. Power
is a double-edged sword, though, and you
could inadvertently hurt someone if you wield
it unconsciously. Play for keeps, but do it with
awareness and humility.

★ **APRIL 22–24**
let freedom ring
Your enthusiasm builds as impetuous Mars
opposes overconfident Jupiter on **April 24**.
Your fervor can take you over the top, but you
may also feel the frustration of Venus squaring
both Mars and Jupiter on **April 23**. Surprisingly,
it's unconventional Uranus that comes to your
rescue as it trines Mars on **April 22**, allowing
you to act independently in a manner that is
not abrasive or obsessive. Instead of rebelling
against a person or an idea, explore your
options with passion and common sense.

★ **APRIL 28**
free falling
An irritating Mars-Neptune quincunx makes
it difficult to know how much force you should
apply to resolve a conflict. Being forthright
won't necessarily help you achieve your goals:
The likelihood of rejection could outweigh the
benefits of disclosure. Once you accept the
lack of clear direction now, the tension could
dissipate, allowing you to move toward resolution over the days ahead.

MAY

RELATIONSHIP STRUGGLES

Venus in sensual Taurus this month reactivates the Grand Earth Trine that influenced your life on **April 18–21**. A quiet satisfaction belies the dramatic intensity beneath the surface, as this trine involves somber Saturn and evolutionary Pluto. Deciding what you want is not a lighthearted affair and can have long-lasting ramifications. But as Mercury dances into flirty Gemini on **May 2**, you find yourself engaging in lively conversations everywhere you go, distracting you from the serious work at hand. Powerful waves are churning as both Saturn and Jupiter change apparent directions in the sky, reinforcing the determined Taurus New Moon on **May 5** in your 7th House of Partners. The New Moon's stressful sesquisquare to immovable Pluto indicates that you may be working at cross purposes with a close friend or partner. Although your tendency is to dig in your heels to resist the winds of change—especially as Mars moves into proud Leo on **May 9**—you will be better served by compromise and a willingness to change your mind.

Both the willful Sun and romantic Venus get boosts of confidence from trines to Jupiter on **May 12 and May 18** as your desires intensify and your mood swings widen and deepen. The passionate Scorpio Full Moon on **May 19** may overwhelm you; making it difficult to know what's real. With Venus square Neptune, your fantasies become so enticing that you may choose them over reality. However, the Sun's entry into cerebral Gemini in your 8th House of Intimacy, combined with the long-term effects of Jupiter's sextile to unconventional Uranus on **May 21**, opens your mind to a whole new array of opportunities ahead.

KEEP IN MIND THIS MONTH

Love may be near, but additional preparation and even sacrifice could be required before you achieve the intimacy you seek.

KEY DATES

★ **MAY 1**
deep connection
You can experience love that truly matters today as Venus harmonizes with passionate Pluto and stabilizing Saturn. Don't miss an opportunity for deep emotional contact, for interactions today will likely have enough substance to withstand the tests of time. Valuable Venus in your 7th House of Others can also be ideal for making an investment, especially if you go in with a partner. Whether in romance or business, you are especially effective as long as you are willing to accept the outer responsibilities while doing the inner work.

★ **MAY 9–11**
back away from the edge
Active Mars is all fired up and ready for the show as it enters expressive Leo on **May 9** in your 10th House of Career. Managing your workload now is critical—don't exhaust yourself. But as Mars quincunxes Pluto on **May 11**, you may be annoyed with the way things are going. Instead

of taking your irritation out on someone at home, channel it into an attack plan for the week ahead. There's no need for a showdown; the tensions will diffuse on their own.

★ **MAY 14**
unreality check
A subtle yet dynamic square from the practical Taurus Sun illuminates dreamy Neptune, luring you into your rich fantasies. You might actually believe that you can be logical enough to think your way through a current relationship or family dilemma, yet the best answers will come from intuitive realizations. Pay attention to your imagination, for spiritual solutions can be just what you need now.

SUPER NOVA DAYS

★ **MAY 19-22**
make a choice
You are standing at a crossroad, and the decisions you make now can have great consequences. The magnetic Scorpio Full Moon on **May 19** infuses you with unresolved emotions. Squares to Saturn and Neptune

suggest that your dreams have escaped from the night and must be reevaluated in the light of day. If you have been overly optimistic, it's time to accept the facts. Still, surprises are possible—even likely—on **May 21**, when the long-lasting sextile is exact between beneficial Jupiter and brilliant Uranus. These are crazy days, but if you're totally carried away by unreachable ideals, the Sun's harsh square with austere Saturn on **May 22** can be an unwelcome reminder of reality.

★ **MAY 26**
be kind to yourself
An unfriendly square between sweet Venus and sobering Saturn can take the wind out of your emotional sails, leaving you without the resources or motivation to finish your journey. With messenger Mercury and dreamer Neptune turning retrograde today, your fears can create an environment where love and communication are withheld. Don't get discouraged; instead, use this time to reconsider what you truly want.

JUNE

STIRRING THE EMOTIONAL STEW

You may find your life overcomplicated by other people's feelings this month. Still, this offers you a chance to engage in the emotional intensity that you crave with the Sun, Venus, and Mercury in your 8th House of Deep Sharing. Thoughtful Mercury, however, is retrograde until **June 19**, reminding you that this awareness is not just about new experiences; remembering old ones can allow you to reconsider them in a new light. The airy Gemini New Moon on **June 3** also falls in your 8th House, emphasizing the mental twist on your typically more emotional posture. Aside from focusing on intimate relationships, consider making a joint financial investment. Just pay close attention to all the details.

You encounter rougher terrain on **June 18** when innocent Venus stands opposite dark Pluto. This emotional tug-of-war draws you deeper into the passions and turmoil of love. You may have to face all-too-familiar control issues as feelings of possessiveness and jealousy are revealed, for the restless Gemini Full Moon conjuncts Pluto the same day. Although life may feel overly intense as you fight for your survival or something you love, you must also consider what needs to be eliminated to support the process of regeneration. Dissatisfaction deepens as long-lasting effects from expansive Jupiter's sesquisquare to restrictive Saturn culminate on **June 26**. But your obsession to reach your goals will give you the strength to overcome any obstacles that now appear in your path, for your two key planets, Mars and Pluto, form a harmonious trine on **June 30**, ending the month with a self-imposed sprint to the finish line, along with an acknowledgment that you are on the road to success.

KEEP IN MIND THIS MONTH

The magic of metamorphosis can only be completed once you eliminate the extra weight of outmoded habits or counterproductive emotional patterns.

KEY DATES

★ **JUNE 7-9**
into the great unknown
An unusual triple conjunction of the Sun, Mercury, and Venus in thinking Gemini falls in your investigative 8th House. This alignment, spread out over three days, increases your innate curiosity enough that you may spend extra energy researching shadowy areas of reality. You could be even more attracted to studying metaphysics or reading about UFOs, near-death experiences, and spirit communication. Give yourself enough time to explore ideas that can deepen your understanding of life's secrets.

★ **JUNE 12-13**
love hangover
Even with the best of spiritual intentions, you may not be able to keep your mind off sex when flirty Venus dynamically squares wild and crazy Uranus in your 5th House of Love on **June 12**. A beautiful fantasy can infuse even the most mundane relationship with a

rejuvenating sense of magic as Venus then trines Neptune on **June 13**. Keep in mind that you don't have to act on everything you can imagine. As much as you love the thrills, you might find yourself outside your usual comfort zone, which can make you feel a bit anxious. Don't worry; this is just a surreal situation, so you might as well revel in it while it lasts.

SUPER NOVA DAYS

★ **JUNE 18–21**
take no prisoners
The adventurous Sagittarius Full Moon on **June 18** is conjunct potent Pluto and brings you more than you bargained for as emotions deepen and sweet love can turn into a battle-field of wills. Intimate relationships become the grounds for difficult transformations, yet you may resist the change. But the Sun opposes Pluto on **June 20** and then slides into emotional Cancer the same day—marking the Summer Solstice—so you must bring these issues to a workable conclusion, whatever the cost. If you cannot resolve the problems, you could feel regret on **June 21** as go-getter Mars

opposes uncertain Neptune. Although you may
be disappointed and less energetic than usual,
this can be a signal to slow down and a reminder
not to push yourself so hard.

★ **JUNE 30**
relentless progress
This annual trine between your two key planets—
warrior Mars in your 10th House of Career and
powerful Pluto—validates your strong commitment to accomplish your goals at work. When
these two fighters combine their forces, your
passions can become compulsive. You must
find ways to express them, or you risk them
erupting with great force. By restraining your
personal quest for power even mildly, you
could greatly increase your odds of getting
what you want. Remember that selfish behavior
will likely backfire on you, so act only for the
greater good.

JULY

SUNNY SIDE OF THE STREET

Opportunities arrive at your doorstep, offering you blue sky and boundless horizons. Paradoxically, however, the month begins on a cautious note, for energetic Mars's range of action is narrowed when it moves into discerning Virgo. Then the nurturing Cancer New Moon on **July 2** falls in your 9th House of Big Ideas and establishes the tone for an over-the-top kind of month. At times, it all looks so good that you're ready to promise anything to make the most of the present moment, yet you must be careful not to let your unbridled passion run roughshod over your common sense.

The theme of overdoing is emphasized as three planets oppose excessive Jupiter, beginning with sweet Venus on **July 3**. Second comes the Sun, on **July 9**, highlighting the positive side of a situation that again can tempt you to be so optimistic that you lose sight of reality. The third opposition to Jupiter in ambitious Capricorn comes from mentally active Mercury on **July 19**. Even the tiniest thought can now grow to grandiose proportions; be watchful for a loss of perspective as you turn molehills into mountains. Fortunately, you will still be feeling the lingering effects of the disciplined Capricorn Full Moon on **July 18**. Balance your overstated intentions with judicious actions and concentrated efforts to bring you closer to your goals. Meanwhile, there is a gradual shift throughout the month that draws all eyes toward you at work with Venus entering proud Leo in your 10th House of Public Status on **July 12**, followed by the Sun on **July 22**, and Mercury on **July 26**. Now is your chance to shine as the leader of the pack.

KEEP IN MIND THIS MONTH

Confidence is healthy, but when unchecked it can lead to trouble. Exercise a bit of self-restraint, especially when everything appears to be going your way.

KEY DATES

★ **JULY 2–3**
life is a cabaret
Fun is in the air. You might find yourself enter-
taining at home with the "family-oriented"
Cancer New Moon conjunct loving Venus.
Additionally, Venus is opposed to joyful Jupiter,
stimulating you to jump in and indulge yourself. Unfortunately, you can easily overspend
or overeat. Since Venus also symbolizes
money, this could be an excellent time to
consider a long-term investment—provided
that your overconfidence doesn't get in the
way of your due diligence.

SUPER NOVA DAYS

★ **JULY 9–10**
metaphysical speed bump
The Sun's opposition to buoyant Jupiter on
July 9 can inspire you to take on more than
you can handle. However, your arrogance is
countered by mental Mercury's opposition to
dark Pluto on **July 10**, triggering the possibility
of a knock-down, drag-out fight to the finish.

83

This difference of opinion is emphasized when "go, go" Mars joins with "no, no" Saturn on the same day, heightening frustration and resentment, especially if your inflexible perspective is extreme. Slowing down and yielding to the opinions of others can help you overcome your dissatisfaction.

★ **JULY 18-19**
give and take
It's challenging for you to find a moderate position right now, with your emotions pulled to extremes by the sensible Capricorn Full Moon opposite the emotional Cancer Sun on **July 18**. Your "all or nothing" approach to relationships may not serve your interests, however; try to find a middle ground. The problem is that bigger isn't necessarily better, though Mercury's tense opposition to giant Jupiter on **July 19** can mislead you to think so. Your best strategy now is to speak your truth and then listen to the response. If you have the courage to talk about your feelings and absorb what is said in return, the path to your future will clear.

★ **JULY 26**
run with it now
A double planetary whammy fires you up as talkative Mercury enters dramatic Leo, prompting you to put your thoughts on the table for all to see. Additionally, a noticeable boost comes from "action hero" Mars's trine to Jupiter, giving you indefatigable energy and unflappable confidence. The Moon in determined Taurus completes a practical Grand Earth Trine involving both Mars and Jupiter, allowing you to apply your efforts efficiently and helping you realize the current potential in your life.

★ **JULY 31**
in love with love
Romantic Venus opposes spiritual Neptune on **July 31**, ending the month on a sweet and gentle note. The biggest danger here is that you can set yourself up for future disappointment, for the Venus-Neptune alignment can make your fantasies seem really real. A reality check now can minimize disillusionment later on.

AUGUST

NO HOLDING BACK

You may not have much choice this month as events draw you into unexpected dramas, precipitating personal transformation. The action begins on **August 1** when a powerful New Moon Eclipse in your 10th House of Career and Community puts an end to the previous cycle of significant growth, initiating a phase of hard work and accountability. Trust your thinking on **August 9**, when mental Mercury harmonizes with Pluto, giving you the ability to concentrate on important matters. You continue to be more organized and efficient throughout the month as Mercury enters its home sign of analytical Virgo on **August 10**, followed by the Sun on **August 22**.

You may not fully understand what's unfolding on the home front on **August 16**, when the emotionally detached Aquarius Full Moon Eclipse in your 4th House of Security is conjunct diffusive Neptune. However, once you accept that it may be beyond rational analysis, you'll be able to glean important spiritual lessons from your experience. Your social life can get a bit crazy as Mercury and Venus oppose Uranus on **August 23**. Excitement in romance, coupled with brilliant debate, can make these days memorable, as long as you don't expect everything to go as planned. Mercury and Venus square Pluto on **August 27 and August 29** before moving into gracious Libra. The intensity heats up one more time as you revisit unresolved power struggles from earlier in the month. If you are willing to go the distance, you can wipe the slate clean and move forward with your life. The down-to-earth Virgo New Moon on **August 30** conjuncts stable Saturn, giving finality to the incredible changes that you have had to face this month.

KEEP IN MIND THIS MONTH

Growth is not painless, and you may be required to give up something dear to move into the next phase of your life. Even the best changes can be difficult at first.

KEY DATES

★ **AUGUST 5–6**
bet on the truth
Innocent Venus forms a harmonious trine to
tough guy Pluto on **August 5**, thrusting you
into an emotionally revealing dance with your
shadow that is likely to be played out through
an intimate relationship. Mars's opposition
to erratic Uranus on **August 6** urges you to
take a risk and deal with the consequences
as they occur. This is a volatile time when deep
tensions can be released. Even if you move
through this phase awkwardly, you will ultimately
realize that the stress is easier to manage once
issues are out in the open.

SUPER NOVA DAYS

★ **AUGUST 13–17**
emotional tug-of-war
The unpredictable Aquarius Full Moon Eclipse
on **August 16** dominates your emotional landscape by reflecting anything you try to avoid.
You may feel restrained by the necessity to
work with others as Venus and Mercury conjunct

restrictive Saturn in your 11th House of Team-work on **August 13–15**, yet you have something important to learn from the group experience. And although Venus and Mercury both trine Jupiter on **August 16–17**—an uplifting and pleasurable aspect—feisty Mars crosses swords with Pluto on **August 17**. This raises the stakes of any conflict and can pit your will against someone else's. Power struggles may be symptomatic of suppressed anger that needs to find constructive expression. Consider the cost of doing battle before you start a fight that increases tension instead of resolving it.

★ **AUGUST 21–23**
open to surprise
A surge of passion washes over you as the impetuous Aries Moon activates a Grand Fire Trine with the Sun and potent Pluto on **August 21**. You are ready to do whatever you must to accomplish your goals and woe to anyone who stands in your way. But the Sun's entry into methodical Virgo on **August 22** could soften your drive. Then, when Mercury

and Venus oppose independent Uranus on
August 23, you are again spurred into action
as your thoughts and feelings flip-flop at the
speed of light. If you're open to the surprising
twists and turns, this can be a wonderful time.
But if you remain inflexible, an overly tense situation could be shattered by sudden change.

★ **AUGUST 27–29**
let it go
Logical Mercury squares Pluto on **August 27**,
demanding that you journey into the hidden
recesses of your mind. Loving Venus repeats
this pattern on **August 29**, turning a curious
intellectual inquiry into an emotional struggle.
The more you try to hold on to an old feeling
or perspective, the more resistance you will
receive. But bringing buried feelings into the
open can positively transform a difficult situation into something promising.

SEPTEMBER

SPIRITUAL RENEWAL

This month begins with four planets in your 12th House of Soul Consciousness, luring you away from the mundane world as you journey inward to seek peace of mind. You are obsessed with discovering the secrets of the cosmos now and may choose to retreat somewhat from the noise of day-to-day life. Finding a healthy balance between your spiritual quest and your ongoing responsibilities is a challenge as the 12th House planets in open-minded Libra square boundless Jupiter. The surge of conviction from this giant planet on **September 7–11** tempts you to throw caution to the wind as you follow your dreams instead of meeting necessary obligations. Fortunately, expansive Jupiter forms the second of three harmonious trines with contractive Saturn on **September 8**, giving you enough common sense to moderate any personal indulgence. You may need some time alone to process your choices consciously. The alternative is just going along with the flow—only to later discover that you missed an important opportunity.

Your desire for solace and escape into fantasy continues as Mercury, Venus, and Mars harmonize with intuitive Neptune on **September 17–22.** Meanwhile, the Sun squares intense Pluto in a clash of wills on **September 20**, just prior to the Autumn Equinox on **September 22** when the Sun enters peace-loving Libra in your 12th House, again reminding you of the importance of walking your spiritual path. The artistic Libra New Moon on **September 29** is awkwardly sesquisquare Neptune, fueling your creative process with images from your dreams. Fortunately, retrograde Mercury's easy trine to Neptune further opens a direct channel into the hidden recesses of your subconscious mind. Listening to your inner voices will give you the guidance needed for what lies ahead.

KEEP IN MIND THIS MONTH

Taking care of your responsibilities must be a part of your spiritual practice. It's not just about finding deeper meaning; it's also about making your life work.

KEY DATES

★ **SEPTEMBER 3–4**
weight of the world
The Sun's annual conjunction with karmic Saturn on **September 3** is usually a time when you should get what you deserve, but this year its trine to generous Jupiter on **September 4** can counteract some of the potential negativity. You are singularly focused and willing to do whatever's necessary to accomplish your goals. With Jupiter's influence, you are fully confident that your actions will have the desired outcome. Still, you can feel the weight of responsibility on your shoulders as you assume more than you can handle. Although you want everyone to acknowledge your significant contribution, keep in mind that exhaustion will only defeat your efforts.

SUPER NOVA DAYS

★ **SEPTEMBER 7–11**
selective service
Work to establish equilibrium between your personal needs and your commitment to others

as abundant Jupiter trines taskmaster Saturn
on **September 8**. Finding balance may not be
easy, for impulsive Mars squares Jupiter on
September 7, filling you with altruism. You are
so eager to help anyone in need that you can
say yes before considering your personal
sacrifice. Then, when fair-minded Mercury
in Libra conjuncts Mars and squares Jupiter
on **September 8**, you can push yourself right
to the edge. Venus repeats this pattern on
September 9–11, again suggesting that discipline and restraint are your keys to success,
so watch those extravagant purchases and
indulgences. Good fortune is indicated as
long as you don't go overboard or overlook any
significant details.

★ **SEPTEMBER 15–17**
emotional challenge
The compassionate Pisces New Moon is zapped
by a high-frequency conjunction to erratic
Uranus on **September 15** in your 5th House
of Children and Romance. Sudden shifts in
your plans may be prompted by a change
in parental responsibilities, or perhaps unex-

pected romantic yearnings will surface that upset the stability of your life. It may be difficult to know what to do with the crazy emotions arising at this time, leaving you unsettled for days to come, especially as loving Venus and logical Mercury form irritating quincunxes with Uranus on **September 16–17**. If you don't feel it in your heart, then inaction is better than false action.

★ **SEPTEMBER 23–24**
spiritual warrior
Your words might turn uncharacteristically surly as Mercury the Communicator and Mars the Warrior join on **September 23** for a second time this month—their first conjunction was on **September 8**—as the Winged Messenger slows down to begin its three-week retrograde phase on **September 24**. This prolongs Mercury's visit to your private 12th House of Endings and encourages you to spend enough time in meditation and contemplation to allow you to complete this current cycle of spiritual growth.

OCTOBER

PHOENIX RISING

Your self-imposed solitude carries forward from last month with the willful Sun, thoughtful Mercury, and self-directed Mars all in your 12th House of Odds and Ends. But this emphasis on your inner world comes to completion as your key planet Mars powers its way into fixed Scorpio on **October 4** and fires up your energy in your 1st House of Physicality. Loving Venus is already in your magnetic sign; Mars's presence there now adds heat and a sense of urgency to your personal expression. The trailblazing Aries Full Moon on **October 14** falls in your 6th House of Health and Work, reflecting a need to change old habits that no longer contribute to your well-being. The daily routine of your job can contribute to boredom, stimulating fantasies about shaking up every-thing. Communicator Mercury turns direct on **October 15**, in your 12th House, giving you a sense of finality before fully emerging from the shadows. The Sun's entry into your sign on **October 22** continues this outgoing trend, lighting up your personality and increasing your self-confidence and charm.

The potent Scorpio New Moon on **October 28** can help you to focus on where you're going and to let go of any recent disappointments that hinder your personal growth. During this lunar cycle, stable Saturn faces off with independent Uranus on **November 4** in the first of five powerful oppositions that could change the direction of your life over the next two years. Meanwhile, Mars's supportive sextile to Saturn and harmonious trine to Uranus on **October 30–31** can surprise you with a very clear idea of how you want to use the power that continues to build in the days ahead.

KEEP IN MIND THIS MONTH

Become more engaged in every aspect of your life.
Although the days may be getting shorter,
your light is growing brighter and your actions
now have major consequences for your future.

KEY DATES

★ **OCTOBER 6**
pull back the reins
Retrograde Mercury passes between the Earth
and the Sun on **October 6** as they both square
powerhouse Jupiter, gracing you with courage.
Your current exuberance can be helpful as
long as you temper any tendency to exaggerate
or overcommit to a social cause. Being aware
of your limitations is a smart practice that will
help you moderate excessive behavior.

★ **OCTOBER 10–11**
delightful surprise
Seductive Venus in Scorpio forms an easy trine
with unorthodox Uranus in your 5th House of
Love and Creativity on **October 10**. On the one
hand, you may be able to successfully persuade
someone into joining your exploration of
unusual interests and unconventional tastes.
On the other, Venus's square to Neptune on
October 11 might have you feeling confused
as you try to integrate unrealistic desires with
your current reality. Nevertheless, this is a

chance to express what you want because your anticipation of breakthrough is greater than your fear of rejection.

★ **OCTOBER 18**
no more drama
It's time to get outside and take in the wonders of nature's beauty as Venus leaves ruminating Scorpio on **October 18** and steps into the adventurous world of Sagittarius. It is easier now for you to move beyond your comfort zone and be more emotionally available. This phase—lasting until **November 12**—also allows you to connect with others through playful flirting and small talk instead of relying on intensity alone.

★ **OCTOBER 24**
paranoia will destroy you
This can be a tumultuous day filled with fierce relationship struggles. Your two key planets, direct Mars and obstinate Pluto, are in a tight semisquare aspect, enabling you to see through someone's social niceties and focus on the underlying issues. But your current

negativity could turn a well-intended act into a fight with no winner. Understanding the other person's motives can help prevent a needless emotional scuffle.

SUPER NOVA DAYS

★ **OCTOBER 27–31**
don't look back

The passionate Scorpio New Moon on **October 28** represents a special passage for you if you can get over your past, for elimination and renewal are difficult unless you're ready to let go of jealousy or anger. But if you are willing to move beyond old wounds, then you can experience the power of regeneration. Fortunately, you receive a boost from Mars as it forms supportive sextiles with buoyant Jupiter on **October 28** and constructive Saturn on **October 30**, followed by an energizing trine with electric Uranus on **October 31**. You are truly in your element now and can accomplish amazing things. Think about what you want to do, for there's no better time to get started than now.

NOVEMBER

PRESENT TENSE,
FUTURE PERFECT

This feels like the month you've been waiting for all year. Although the stress may be overwhelming at times, you are hopeful about the potential that exists all around you. You might not know the best way to move through the current obstacles, but if you take it one step at a time, you can set a foundation in stone upon which you can build your life for a long time to come. The dilemma, however, is the first of five oppositions between stabilizing Saturn and destabilizing Uranus on **November 4**. This powerful long-term cycle will last until **July 2010**. If you hang back in fear, rigid structures can buckle under the pressure. The ground may shift beneath your feet, but if you assume a flexible attitude, your life will withstand the shaking and rattling—and be better off for it.

Fortunately, buoyant Jupiter relieves the tension as its sextiles Uranus on **November 13** and trines Saturn on **November 21**. Jupiter's supportive sextile to Uranus is the third and the last of this series—the first was on **March 28**, the second on **May 21**—continuing to open your mind to new possibilities and exciting opportunities. Good news may arrive out of the blue, giving you possible solutions where none previously existed. Encouraging Jupiter and discouraging Saturn, the cosmic regulators, have been holding your life in balance somewhere between expansion and contraction, so prepare to put your ideas into motion when Jupiter trines Saturn. It's time to look back over the last couple of years to see what gains you've made and what lessons you've learned. It's essential now to build on your past efforts rather than hastily acting on impulse with something new.

KEEP IN MIND THIS MONTH

Instead of worrying whether you are on the right track, keep one eye on the past, one eye on the future, and your feet grounded in the present circumstances.

KEY DATES

SUPER NOVA DAYS

★ **NOVEMBER 3–4**
no solution in sight

The long-term opposition between immovable Saturn and irrepressible Uranus on **November 4** can increase stress levels regarding money and love, especially as valuable Venus dynamically squares both planets on **November 3**. You cannot easily hide your displeasure: You want something more than you have, and there may not be a simple path to your heart's desire. Extreme actions—whether purposefully hiding your true feelings or suddenly demanding that your needs be met now—may not have the desired effects. Don't push for resolution yet; just get the issues out into the open. The stakes increase as communicator Mercury enters probing Scorpio, also on **November 4**, remaining in your sign until **November 23**. Additionally, self-directed Mars squares dreamy Neptune the same day, intensifying the conflict between your current situation and your spiritual inclinations. Gather all the knowledge you can now, Scorpio, to help you make the big decisions looming on the horizon.

★ **NOVEMBER 12–16**
who do you trust?
Love becomes a temporary battleground of raw emotions as vulnerable Venus engages in an intense power struggle with your key planet Pluto on **November 12**. But instead of being overwhelmed by someone else's passions, the hopeful Jupiter-Uranus sextile on **November 13** allows you to clear a path to a higher expression of love. A stubborn Taurus Full Moon squares Neptune the same day, signaling that your common sense clashes with your intuition. Fortunately, the confusion dissipates and clarity returns when mental Mercury harmonizes with Uranus, Jupiter, and Saturn on **November 16**. Ultimately, it's best to trust your own thoughts now over the counsel of anyone else.

★ **NOVEMBER 21–23**
into the great wide open
The easy trine between stable Saturn and visionary Jupiter on **November 21** gives you

the ability to organize what you know into a sensible plan of action. It's easier for you to see what's ahead as the Sun and Mercury leave compulsive Scorpio for the more inspirational and philosophical realms of Sagittarius on **November 21 and November 23**, respectively. The change is noticeable, and you must consciously shift your vision from the past to focus with hope on the future in order to best capture the potential of this moment.

★ **NOVEMBER 27–29**
holiday spice
The high-spirited Sagittarius New Moon on Thanksgiving, **November 27**, joins Mercury and Mars in bringing a fun-loving intensity to your holiday weekend. Your festive mood grows as Venus harmonizes with the Uranus-Saturn opposition on **November 28–29**, calming their conflict between freedom and responsibility. Fortunately, a realistic attitude about money and love during this time can inspire you to make sound investments for your future.

DECEMBER

AFTER THE DELUGE

On **December 1**, a lovely conjunction between pleasant Venus and opulent Jupiter indicates a kinder, gentler month ahead. Your good feelings may not last long, though, for big-talking Mercury, energetic Mars, and the Sun—now all moving through adventurous Sagittarius—square the waning Saturn-Uranus opposition that was exact last month. Mental Mercury squares irrepressible Uranus on **December 5** and restrictive Saturn on **December 6**, signaling that your brilliant ideas could run into an obstacle. The Sun squares Uranus on **December 10** and Saturn on **December 12** as you act impulsively and then reconsider your actions a bit too late. But Mars's square to Uranus on **December 12** overrides common sense, and you rebel against the current restrictions regardless of the consequences. The Gemini Full Moon on the same day increases the hype, heightens the instability, and—with Mercury's conjunction to Pluto—intensifies all forms of communication. Your frustrations may still be running high as feisty Mars squares authoritative Saturn on **December 15**, requiring you to cool your heels, reassess your present circumstances, and then move ahead with caution.

As the holiday spirit picks you up, the dust should settle as three planets exit cavalier Sagittarius and enter conservative Capricorn. Your thinking becomes more pragmatic as Mercury enters Capricorn on **December 12**, followed by the Sun on **December 21** and Mars on **December 27**. The tradition-oriented Capricorn New Moon on **December 27** falls in your 4th House of Roots, enabling you to spend quality time with those you love; this also marks the beginning of an ambitious phase as you work hard to integrate your recent experiences and create your strategy for the year to come.

KEEP IN MIND THIS MONTH

Managing your stress through the holidays is crucial. If you take care of each situation as it arises, you will have time to partake in the festivities as well.

KEY DATES

★ **DECEMBER 5–6**
cruising for trouble
The Sun's conjunction with "superhero" Mars on **December 5** illuminates your ability to fight for your basic values, but your indefatigable energy runs into a wall, creating a messy situation. You are hot for action, and tempers can flare with communicator Mercury being provoked by a square from rebellious Uranus. But you cannot just walk away from issues once they've been stirred up, for Mercury squares stern Saturn on **December 6**, insisting that you answer to authority—whether it be your boss, your spouse, or your own conscience.

SUPER NOVA DAY

★ **DECEMBER 12**
true confessions
The restless Gemini Full Moon in your 8th House of Intimacy and Shared Resources can fill your life with stressful changes affecting both money and love. Although Mars squares erratic Uranus, driving you to the edge of

frustration, suppression is not the answer.
Your ruling planet Pluto is joined by the heavenly
messenger Mercury, giving wings to your
deepest thoughts. They can pack a punch,
though, when they erupt into conversation.
It won't be easy to overcome your inertia with
restrictive Saturn squaring your Sun. But you
must express your truth, and it's better to do
it gently and preemptively instead of waiting
for someone else to provoke it.

★ **DECEMBER 21-22**
point of no return
The Winter Solstice on **December 21**, marked
by the Sun's entry into hardworking Capricorn,
can be a significant turning point for you,
especially if you set your heart on a goal and
commit to achieving it. You cannot go back
once the Sun joins transformative Pluto on
December 22 and deepens your resolve.
Fortunately, your fierce passion will give you
the strength you need. Since the Sun-Pluto
conjunction in your 3rd House of Communication
shines light on whatever is no longer needed,
you may have to give up a belief you once

considered important. Don't hold on to a
grudge or insecurity that no longer has any
purpose. And remember that your current
actions may have much greater impact now
than you realize.

★ **DECEMBER 28–31**
purposeful and powerful
Mars's conjunction with intense Pluto on
December 28 reactivates old fears of being
forced to do something against your will.
You are ready to take a stand, even if it means
raining on the holiday parade. You are quite
serious and filled with a sense of purpose, so
you cannot go along for the ride unless it's
heading in your direction. Fortunately, interac-
tive Mercury comes to the rescue just in time
for the New Year's celebrations as it joins jolly
Jupiter on **December 30**. Release all negativity
and fear so you can ring in your future on a
happier note.

APPENDIXES

★

2008 MONTH-AT-A-GLANCE ASTROCALENDAR

★

FAMOUS SCORPIOS

★

SCORPIO IN LOVE

TUESDAY 1

WEDNESDAY 2 ★ **SUPER NOVA DAY** Confront issues in a fight to the finish

THURSDAY 3

FRIDAY 4

SATURDAY 5

SUNDAY 6

MONDAY 7

TUESDAY 8

WEDNESDAY 9 ★ Even the most magical thoughts can be applied to the real world

THURSDAY 10 ★

FRIDAY 11 ★

SATURDAY 12 ★

SUNDAY 13 ★

MONDAY 14

TUESDAY 15

WEDNESDAY 16

THURSDAY 17

FRIDAY 18

SATURDAY 19 ★ Build a bridge instead of a wall through the 21st

SUNDAY 20 ★

MONDAY 21 ★

TUESDAY 22 ★ Take a walk on the dark side through the 24th

WEDNESDAY 23 ★

THURSDAY 24 ★

FRIDAY 25

SATURDAY 26

SUNDAY 27

MONDAY 28

TUESDAY 29

WEDNESDAY 30

THURSDAY 31

FRIDAY 1 ★ Put off big decisions, but look to inner voices for guidance through the 2nd

---

SATURDAY 2 ★

SUNDAY 3

MONDAY 4

TUESDAY 5

WEDNESDAY 6 ★ **SUPER NOVA DAYS** Change the rules through the 7th

---

THURSDAY 7 ★

FRIDAY 8

SATURDAY 9

SUNDAY 10

MONDAY 11

TUESDAY 12

WEDNESDAY 13 ★ A gesture of reconciliation goes far now

THURSDAY 14 ★

FRIDAY 15

SATURDAY 16

SUNDAY 17

MONDAY 18

TUESDAY 19

WEDNESDAY 20 ★ Choose logic over the whims of your heart

THURSDAY 21

FRIDAY 22

SATURDAY 23

SUNDAY 24 ★ Rise to the challenge of meeting your goals step by step

---

MONDAY 25

TUESDAY 26

WEDNESDAY 27

THURSDAY 28

FRIDAY 29

SATURDAY 1

SUNDAY 2

MONDAY 3

TUESDAY 4

WEDNESDAY 5

THURSDAY 6 ★ **SUPER NOVA DAYS** Passions are heightened through the 8th

FRIDAY 7 ★

SATURDAY 8 ★

SUNDAY 9

MONDAY 10

TUESDAY 11

WEDNESDAY 12

THURSDAY 13

FRIDAY 14 ★ Find healthy outlets to decrease pressure through the 18th

SATURDAY 15 ★

SUNDAY 16 ★

MONDAY 17 ★

TUESDAY 18 ★

WEDNESDAY 19

THURSDAY 20

FRIDAY 21 ★ Manage your conflicts without fanning the fires

SATURDAY 22

SUNDAY 23

MONDAY 24

TUESDAY 25

WEDNESDAY 26

THURSDAY 27

FRIDAY 28 ★ Confidence gives you a magnetic appeal through the 30th

SATURDAY 29 ★

SUNDAY 30 ★

MONDAY 31

TUESDAY 1	
WEDNESDAY 2	
THURSDAY 3 ★ Make positive changes through the 6th before you boil over	

FRIDAY 4 ★	
SATURDAY 5 ★	
SUNDAY 6 ★	
MONDAY 7	
TUESDAY 8	
WEDNESDAY 9	
THURSDAY 10 ★ Watch your aggression—your reactions may be out of proportion	

FRIDAY 11	
SATURDAY 12	
SUNDAY 13	
MONDAY 14	
TUESDAY 15	
WEDNESDAY 16	
THURSDAY 17	
FRIDAY 18 ★ **SUPER NOVA DAYS** Use power with intent through the 21st	

SATURDAY 19 ★	
SUNDAY 20 ★	
MONDAY 21 ★	
TUESDAY 22 ★ Explore freedom with passion and reason through the 24th	

WEDNESDAY 23 ★	
THURSDAY 24 ★	
FRIDAY 25	
SATURDAY 26	
SUNDAY 27	
MONDAY 28 ★ Accept your lack of clear direction and tension will dissipate	

TUESDAY 29	
WEDNESDAY 30	

THURSDAY 1 ★ A deep connection made today will likely stand the test of time

---

FRIDAY 2

SATURDAY 3

SUNDAY 4

MONDAY 5

TUESDAY 6

WEDNESDAY 7

THURSDAY 8

FRIDAY 9 ★ Back away from the edge to diffuse tensions through the 11th

---

SATURDAY 10 ★

SUNDAY 11 ★

MONDAY 12

TUESDAY 13

WEDNESDAY 14 ★ The best answers come from intuitive realizations

---

THURSDAY 15

FRIDAY 16

SATURDAY 17

SUNDAY 18

MONDAY 19 ★ **SUPER NOVA DAYS** Make an important decision by the 22nd

---

TUESDAY 20 ★

WEDNESDAY 21 ★

THURSDAY 22 ★

FRIDAY 23

SATURDAY 24

SUNDAY 25

MONDAY 26 ★ Be kind to yourself and reconsider what you truly want

---

TUESDAY 27

WEDNESDAY 28

THURSDAY 29

FRIDAY 30

SATURDAY 31

SUNDAY 1

MONDAY 2

TUESDAY 3

WEDNESDAY 4

THURSDAY 5

FRIDAY 6

SATURDAY 7 ★ Venture into the spiritual unknown through the 9th

SUNDAY 8 ★

MONDAY 9 ★

TUESDAY 10

WEDNESDAY 11

THURSDAY 12 ★ Revel in your beautiful fantasies through the 13th

FRIDAY 13 ★

SATURDAY 14

SUNDAY 15

MONDAY 16

TUESDAY 17

WEDNESDAY 18 ★ **SUPER NOVA DAYS**
Take no prisoners through the 21st

THURSDAY 19 ★

FRIDAY 20 ★

SATURDAY 21 ★

SUNDAY 22

MONDAY 23

TUESDAY 24

WEDNESDAY 25

THURSDAY 26

FRIDAY 27

SATURDAY 28

SUNDAY 29

MONDAY 30 ★ Relentless progress is the result of passion

TUESDAY 1

WEDNESDAY 2 ★ Avoid overspending on yourself through the 3rd

THURSDAY 3 ★

FRIDAY 4

SATURDAY 5

SUNDAY 6

MONDAY 7

TUESDAY 8

WEDNESDAY 9 ★ **SUPER NOVA DAYS** Slow down through the 10th

THURSDAY 10 ★

FRIDAY 11

SATURDAY 12

SUNDAY 13

MONDAY 14

TUESDAY 15

WEDNESDAY 16

THURSDAY 17

FRIDAY 18 ★ Try to find a middle ground in relationships through the 19th

SATURDAY 19 ★

SUNDAY 20

MONDAY 21

TUESDAY 22

WEDNESDAY 23

THURSDAY 24

FRIDAY 25

SATURDAY 26 ★ Run with your energy and unflappable confidence

SUNDAY 27

MONDAY 28

TUESDAY 29

WEDNESDAY 30

THURSDAY 31 ★ A reality check can minimize later disappointment in love

FRIDAY 1	
SATURDAY 2	
SUNDAY 3	
MONDAY 4	
TUESDAY 5 ★	Take a risk and deal with the consequences through the 6th
WEDNESDAY 6 ★	
THURSDAY 7	
FRIDAY 8	
SATURDAY 9	
SUNDAY 10	
MONDAY 11	
TUESDAY 12	
WEDNESDAY 13 ★	**SUPER NOVA DAYS** Consider the cost of battle through the 17th
THURSDAY 14 ★	
FRIDAY 15 ★	
SATURDAY 16 ★	
SUNDAY 17 ★	
MONDAY 18	
TUESDAY 19	
WEDNESDAY 20	
THURSDAY 21 ★	If you're open to surprise, you'll have a wonderful time through the 23rd
FRIDAY 22 ★	
SATURDAY 23 ★	
SUNDAY 24	
MONDAY 25	
TUESDAY 26	
WEDNESDAY 27 ★	Let go of old feelings and perspectives through the 29th
THURSDAY 28 ★	
FRIDAY 29 ★	
SATURDAY 30	
SUNDAY 31	

MONDAY 1

TUESDAY 2

WEDNESDAY 3 ★ You may feel the weight of the world on your back through the 4th

THURSDAY 4 ★

FRIDAY 5

SATURDAY 6

SUNDAY 7 ★ **SUPER NOVA DAYS**
Be selective with your altruism through the 11th

MONDAY 8 ★

TUESDAY 9 ★

WEDNESDAY 10 ★

THURSDAY 11 ★

FRIDAY 12

SATURDAY 13

SUNDAY 14

MONDAY 15 ★ Trust your heart when emotional challenges rise through the 17th

TUESDAY 16 ★

WEDNESDAY 17 ★

THURSDAY 18

FRIDAY 19

SATURDAY 20

SUNDAY 21

MONDAY 22

TUESDAY 23 ★ Meditation and contemplation help you grow spiritually
through the 24th

WEDNESDAY 24★

THURSDAY 25

FRIDAY 26

SATURDAY 27

SUNDAY 28

MONDAY 29

TUESDAY 30

WEDNESDAY 1	
THURSDAY 2	
FRIDAY 3	
SATURDAY 4	
SUNDAY 5	
MONDAY 6 ★	Pull back the reins before you overcommit
TUESDAY 7	
WEDNESDAY 8	
THURSDAY 9	
FRIDAY 10 ★	Explore unusual interests through the 11th
SATURDAY 11 ★	
SUNDAY 12	
MONDAY 13	
TUESDAY 14	
WEDNESDAY 15	
THURSDAY 16	
FRIDAY 17	
SATURDAY 18 ★	Move beyond your comfort zone to become emotionally available
SUNDAY 19	
MONDAY 20	
TUESDAY 21	
WEDNESDAY 22	
THURSDAY 23	
FRIDAY 24 ★	Don't succumb to paranoia during relationship struggles
SATURDAY 25	
SUNDAY 26	
MONDAY 27 ★ **SUPER NOVA DAYS**	Don't look back now
TUESDAY 28 ★	
WEDNESDAY 29 ★	
THURSDAY 30 ★	
FRIDAY 31	

SATURDAY 1

SUNDAY 2

MONDAY 3 ★ **SUPER NOVA DAYS**
There's no easy solution in sight through the 4th

TUESDAY 4 ★

WEDNESDAY 5

THURSDAY 6

FRIDAY 7

SATURDAY 8

SUNDAY 9

MONDAY 10

TUESDAY 11

WEDNESDAY 12 ★ Trust your own thoughts over anyone else through the 16th

THURSDAY 13 ★

FRIDAY 14 ★

SATURDAY 15 ★

SUNDAY 16 ★

MONDAY 17

TUESDAY 18

WEDNESDAY 19

THURSDAY 20

FRIDAY 21 ★ Venture into the great wide open through the 23rd

SATURDAY 22 ★

SUNDAY 23 ★

MONDAY 24

TUESDAY 25

WEDNESDAY 26

THURSDAY 27 ★ The holidays are spiced with fun-loving intensity

FRIDAY 28 ★

SATURDAY 29 ★

SUNDAY 30

MONDAY 1	
TUESDAY 2	
WEDNESDAY 3	
THURSDAY 4	
FRIDAY 5 ★	Trouble lurks if you don't answer to authority now

SATURDAY 6 ★	
SUNDAY 7	
MONDAY 8	
TUESDAY 9	
WEDNESDAY 10	
THURSDAY 11	
FRIDAY 12 ★	**SUPER NOVA DAY** True confessions pack a punch

SATURDAY 13	
SUNDAY 14	
MONDAY 15	
TUESDAY 16	
WEDNESDAY 17	
THURSDAY 18	
FRIDAY 19	
SATURDAY 20	
SUNDAY 21 ★	Let go of grudges through the 22nd

MONDAY 22 ★	
TUESDAY 23	
WEDNESDAY 24	
THURSDAY 25	
FRIDAY 26	
SATURDAY 27	
SUNDAY 28 ★	Take a purposeful and powerful stand through the 31st

MONDAY 29 ★	
TUESDAY 30 ★	
WEDNESDAY 31 ★	

FAMOUS SCORPIOS

Michael Crichton	★	10/23/1942
Johnny Carson	★	10/23/1925
Pelé	★	10/23/1940
Kevin Kline	★	10/24/1947
Minnie Pearl	★	10/25/1912
Pablo Picasso	★	10/25/1881
Hillary Rodham Clinton	★	10/26/1947
Mahalia Jackson	★	10/26/1911
Dylan Thomas	★	10/27/1914
Roy Lichtenstein	★	10/27/1923
Theodore Roosevelt	★	10/27/1858
Julia Roberts	★	10/28/1967
Jonas Salk	★	10/28/1914
Bill Gates	★	10/28/1955
Winona Ryder	★	10/29/1971
Fanny Brice	★	10/29/1891
Grace Slick	★	10/30/1939
Ezra Pound	★	10/30/1885
John Adams	★	10/30/1735
Peter Jackson	★	10/31/1961
Jan Vermeer	★	10/31/1632
Larry Flynt	★	11/1/1942
Marie Antoinette	★	11/2/1755
Pat Buchanan	★	11/2/1938
k.d. lang	★	11/2/1961
Charles Bronson	★	11/3/1921
Roseanne	★	11/3/1952
Laura Bush	★	11/4/1946
Sean "Diddy" Combs	★	11/4/1969
Walter Cronkite	★	11/4/1916
Vivien Leigh	★	11/5/1913
Art Garfunkel	★	11/5/1941
Tatum O'Neal	★	11/5/1963
Ethan Hawke	★	11/6/1970
Sally Field	★	11/6/1946

FAMOUS SCORPIOS

Rebecca Romijn	★	11/6/1972
Leon Trotsky	★	11/7/1879
Joni Mitchell	★	11/7/1943
Bonnie Raitt	★	11/8/1949
Parker Posey	★	11/8/1968
Margaret Mitchell	★	11/8/1900
Richard Burton	★	11/10/1925
Kurt Vonnegut, Jr.	★	11/11/1922
Demi Moore	★	11/11/1962
Fyodor Dostoyevsky	★	11/11/1821
Sammy Sosa	★	11/12/1968
Grace Kelly	★	11/12/1929
Nadia Comaneci	★	11/12/1961
Neil Young	★	11/12/1945
Robert Louis Stevenson	★	11/13/1850
Whoopi Goldberg	★	11/13/1955
Claude Monet	★	11/14/1840
Prince Charles	★	11/14/1948
Veronica Lake	★	11/14/1919
Georgia O'Keeffe	★	11/15/1887
Rock Hudson	★	11/17/1925
Martin Scorsese	★	11/17/1942
RuPaul	★	11/17/1960
Linda Evans	★	11/18/1942
Calvin Klein	★	11/19/1942
Indira Gandhi	★	11/19/1917
Jodie Foster	★	11/19/1962
Meg Ryan	★	11/19/1961
Bo Derek	★	11/20/1956
Robert F. Kennedy	★	11/20/1925
Bjork	★	11/21/1965
Goldie Hawn	★	11/21/1945
Voltaire	★	11/21/1694
Ken Griffey, Jr.	★	11/21/1969

SCORPIO IN LOVE

SCORPIO–ARIES (MARCH 21–APRIL 19)

A super achiever, you project yourself with willpower and sheer passion. Your Aries partner is hard driving, and thrives on excitement and independence. Both signs are ruled by Mars, the Greek god of war, and are therefore endowed with personal willpower and courage. You can endure strong emotions by holding them inward, transforming them from the inside out; Aries has a shorter fuse and tends toward sudden outbursts. Compared to your pensive and sometimes sullen personality, your lover is quicker to forgive and forget than you are. These character traits mix like oil and water, but if the tension is converted to sexual passion, the power unleashed can rock both your worlds. Your chances for success will be greatly increased if the Moon in your chart is in a fire or air sign, lightening your emotional load. Also, if your Mercury or Venus is in Sagittarius, then you won't feel so overwhelmed by the heat of your impulsive Ram. If the two of you can move toward a higher consciousness and get beyond the personality traps of your signs, you'll have a chance to create a long-lasting relationship full of love and passion.

SCORPIO–TAURUS (APRIL 20–MAY 20)

You are passionate and sincere when it comes to relationships and sexuality. You need intensity and take pleasure in showering your mate with affection. Yet if you feel double-crossed, insulted, or otherwise emotionally wounded, it may take several lifetimes for you to forgive your lover. In Taurus, you find someone who's trustworthy and has basic, simple needs. Taurus is steadfast and sensual. Occupying the opposite zone of the zodiacal wheel, your Bull loves to be on the receiving end of your intense passions. The two of you will spoil each other, thoroughly enjoying the experience as long as you maintain the status quo regarding relationship needs. This is a delicate balance—trouble can quickly brew if you two fixed signs have power struggles over dominance. You each make a worthy adversary if it comes to that—a showdown between the two of you would be ugly. Other problems may arise if you feel restrained by the down-to-earth simplicity of your Taurus mate, unless you have the Moon or Venus in an earth sign. The good news is that together you have a strong flair for romance. The trick will be how to maintain balance and if you can do this, it can be very satisfying and rewarding for both of you.

SCORPIO-GEMINI (MAY 21–JUNE 20)

You love to solve mysteries and delve deeply into the affairs of others, sometimes even without their knowledge. You are a natural detective who enjoys unraveling a puzzle, which is partly why you're drawn toward suspense and emotional drama. The keen intellect and sharp wit of your Gemini partner appreciates these qualities in you and may actually enjoy sharing ideas and debating issues with you, but they are no match for your intensity. In fact, you just may scare the heck out of them. While Gemini is attracted to the display of fireworks, you're more concerned with what's fueling the volcano. You just may be too serious for Gemini. If, however, your chart has the Moon in an air sign or if Venus is in Libra or Sagittarius, compatibility is more likely. Your clever Gemini may have a half-passionate, half-intellectual approach to affairs of the heart—creating a romantic interlude that includes discussions about the unknown mysteries of life. The biggest obstacle that you'll need to overcome is that your Gemini mate is flighty and casually flirtatious, which will stir up your issues of possessiveness and jealousy. You'll each have some adjustments to make in order to create a harmonious relationship.

SCORPIO–CANCER (JUNE 21–JULY 22)

As a water sign, you're highly sensitive to undercurrents in your environment, and are able to detect people's moods with your probing mind. Cancer is also a water sign who expresses feelings and moods with greater unpredictability than you. You both tend to hold in your emotions, but for different reasons. Yours are so powerful that you often tone them down so as not to scare others, while your Cancer mate can hide feelings under a hard outer shell. He or she worries that sharing emotions will scare loved ones away, so you will need to build trust. You can teach your mate to have courage and self-confidence. Meanwhile, the Crab's nurturing character coaxes your own suppressed emotions out of hiding. Your lover can be highly expressive sexually, but may be more hesitant than you; just be patient and tender. Differences of style can get in the way of daily routines if the Moon in your chart is in Aries, Libra, Sagittarius, or Aquarius. Regardless of the Moon's placement, you enjoy each other's company and may enjoy spending quality time near the ocean. If the two of you choose to create a home together it will be full of strong emotions, yet it can ultimately turn into a private haven from the outside world.

SCORPIO–LEO (JULY 23–AUGUST 22)

Chances are that you're an accomplished individual who needs to feel productive and respected within your sphere. You take pride in your efforts to meet the needs of the community and are often employed in jobs that are risky and intense, requiring specific skills combined with courage. There are many police officers, firefighters, and doctors who are born under the influence of Scorpio. Leos are also deeply sincere in their efforts, but they tend to be more grandiose and flamboyant in the outer world, sometimes grabbing the limelight away from less showy signs. If your Leo underestimates your value by stealing attention or making light of your worth, you'll find it intolerable and probably cut off the relationship. You and your Leo lover are both fixed signs, and therefore can be quite stubborn in your own individual ways. Unless you have the Moon or Mars in a fire sign, you may see your partner as someone who wastes energy on the wrong things. Even with other compatible planets, this relationship is fraught with tension. You'll need to compromise in significant ways and learn to respect each other's differences. If you can do this, your mutual sense of loyalty can help forge a lasting union.

SCORPIO–VIRGO (AUGUST 23–SEPT. 22)

You have a deep, personal interest in transformation and healing, drawing on inner power to overcome emotional or physical trauma. It's as if you can transcend the boundaries of everyday living and mundane thought forms. When you put your mind to something, you can soar like an eagle, letting go of old patterns and experiencing self-empowerment from rebirth. Like you, your Virgo mate has a wealth of resources, and will exert this power inwardly in order to overcome obstacles and challenges. Virgo's energy is more analytical and practical than yours. You tend to be more emotional and raw, unless your Moon or Mars is in an earth sign, grounding your feelings and increasing compatibility. There's a deep respect between you and your partner and together you can make great work allies, as you appreciate the careful order from which Virgo conducts the everyday routines of life. Romantically, you're both too hot for many people, and although your lover may seem cool and detached, he or she can focus passion like a laser. If this love light shines your way, you two can cultivate long-lasting and mutually satisfying rhythms and routines that withstand the test of time.

SCORPIO–LIBRA (SEPT. 23–OCT. 22)

You enjoy the seclusion of peaceful surroundings, which can help soothe your passions. You're private in your romantic and home life—often remaining reserved, even secretive, in the early stages of intimacy. Your Libran can add an artistic refinement to your environment and can help you find ways to balance your head and your heart. He or she will probably be more social than you, approaching life from an intellectually based set of sensibilities, while you feel things without necessarily putting words to them. Libra uses language and actions to create pleasantness, and can make an excellent host or hostess. The question is: Do you want someone to make things nice? Or do you want someone who can engage your tumultuous passions? If you have Venus in Libra, compatibility is increased. If your Moon is in any air sign (Gemini, Libra, or Aquarius), you'll be more accepting of your mate's artistic gifts. Even without this support from other planets, Libra can be a suitable match for you. If you allow, lovely Libra can lead you into a more gentle way of living, while you return sincere and lasting love. Together you can share an abiding trust from which you explore the virtues of pleasure and the finer things in life.

SCORPIO–SCORPIO (OCT. 23–NOV. 21)

You are interested in all the untold secrets of the universe, especially those involving transformation. You tend to be complex as you seek to merge the physical and spiritual realms. You can either be extremely honest and honorable or revengeful, judging, and manipulative. For you, there is rarely a middle ground. When you meet another Scorpio, it's possible you will immediately dislike each other at first. Powerful passions and fears come to the surface, bringing up issues of intimacy and control. You can be powerful mirrors to each other and you may not like seeing yourself so closely. There can be strong attraction, but as you see yourself from a different viewpoint, you may be astounded at how intense you are. The placement in your chart of Mars, your ruling planet, is key. If it's compatible with your lover's chart, this union can be most successful. At times, the intensity may be so great that you'll feel a need for time apart, which is healthy and advised. Learn to get past petty jealousies and arguments— try bringing humor into the relationship. Because of the physical and emotional intensity, strong sexuality issues can manifest; you'll each need courage and trust to push through whatever comes.

SCORPIO–SAGITTARIUS (NOV. 22–DEC. 21)

You Scorpios have a keen sense of financial strategy, preferring to manage money matters with dignified intelligence. You can be brutally truthful and have great integrity in business, no matter what the cost. When you combine your management capabilities and street savvy with optimistic and truth-oriented Sagittarius, there is tremendous chemistry and mutual respect. The biggest conflict is that your intuition is emotionally based, while your Archer shoots from the hip and can enthusiastically swing into action, riding roughshod over your objections. Sagittarius can become impatient with your need to process emotions. On the other hand, you'll grow weary of your lover's avoidance of unpleasant or dark feelings. Your chance for optimum compatibility is improved if the Moon in your chart is in a fire or air sign. Sagittarians are adventurous and active. Their irrepressible confidence is inspiring. The lovable Archer can offer humor to your sometimes overly serious ways. Meanwhile, you add passion to the relationship as you push your mate into deeper emotional, spiritual, and philosophical realms. Allowing for your differences, you can make this union successful, and complement each other well.

SCORPIO–CAPRICORN (DEC. 22–JAN. 19)

Privacy and self-preservation play a significant role in your life. You aren't inclined to casually blurt out feelings or opinions when in the company of groups, new friends, or professional settings. However intense your feelings, you keep your thoughts to yourself—revealing little of your internal life until you fully trust the people around you. Capricorns display similar behavior, although for different reasons. They, too, portray a reserved demeanor, but for the Goat, it's about doing what is right. Sharing feelings in many situations is just inappropriate for them no matter what the motivation—you and your Capricorn respect each other's personal space. Unless you have the Moon or Venus in an earth sign, you might find the Goat too dry and lacking of emotion. But don't let that cool exterior fool you. Capricorn learns the steps and then can dance with total abandon. As you teach your lover how to explore the depths of feelings, he or she will follow your lead. Capricorns are special lovers preferring private displays of affection and sensuality. You two can have great chemistry, and the sex can register high on the Richter scale. If you're both open with your feelings, this can be a lasting, loving union.

SCORPIO-AQUARIUS (JAN. 20–FEB. 18)

You want a home environment that reflects your need for depth and privacy, a place where you can safely express your passions with your lover. Your Aquarius partner needs a more communal life, preferring more casual interactions with additional people. This difference in approach to life can stop this relationship right in its tracks before it ever leaves the station. If, however, you both meet in the middle, you may together create a most interesting life—one that is filled with eccentric and individual taste. Together, you'll prefer to host people in your home rather than venturing out into other people's territory. In this way, you get to experience the safety and integrity of your social world as you define it and your Aquarius mate is able to bring his or her need for additional interactions to the home hearth. You're both fixed signs and can be stubborn to the core. You'll need to stay vigilant on this issue to avoid slipping into power struggles. It'll help if Venus in your chart is in Libra or Sagittarius. Your possessive tendencies may feel restrictive to your independent Aquarius lover. Trust is key in this relationship. This isn't an easy pairing, but you can achieve happiness if you can offer each other room to be who you are.

SCORPIO-PISCES (FEB. 19–MARCH 20)

You can be extremely attentive to your partner's emotional needs as long as you are able to say what you feel—and that means you need to feel safe and secure. You have a tendency to be possessive and jealous, especially if you've suffered rejection and/or abandonment in the past. Pisces, another water sign, is emotionally sensitive and compassionate, often preferring to relate with those who understand the mystical treasures of life. Your Pisces lover has a kind heart and can sooth your intense emotions, lending a tender understanding to the plight of your life trials. Although you're both emotionally oriented, you're more involved in processing personal feelings. Pisces tend to spiritualize feelings, turning passion into compassion. Still, they can be easily bruised by your emotional outbursts. You'll need to learn to be softer and they'll need to toughen up a bit. If your Moon's in Gemini, Leo, Libra, or Sagittarius, you may find it difficult to understand dreamy Pisces. You can strengthen the life path of your Pisces partner as they watch you demonstrate the inward focus and resourcefulness that you possess. This can be a wonderful match and your imaginative Pisces lover can offer you the keys to a sensual love life.

ABOUT THE AUTHORS

♏

RICK LEVINE When I first encountered astrology as a psychology undergraduate in the late 1960s, I became fascinated with the varieties of human experience. Even now, I love the one-on-one work of seeing clients and looking at their lives through the cosmic lens. But I also love history and utilize astrology to better understand the longer-term cycles of cultural change. My recent DVD, *Quantum Astrology*, explores some of these transpersonal interests. As a scientist, I'm always looking for patterns in order to improve my ability to predict the outcome of any experiment; as an artist, I'm entranced by the mystery of what we do not and cannot know. As an astrologer, I am privileged to live in an enchanted world that links the rational and magical, physical and spiritual—and yes—even science and art.

JEFF JAWER I'm a Taurus with a Scorpio Moon and Aries rising who lives in the Pacific Northwest with Danick, my double-Pisces wife, our two very well-behaved teenage Leo daughters, and two black Gemini cats (who are not so well-behaved). I have been a professional astrologer since 1973. I encountered astrology as my first marriage was ending. I was searching and needed to understand myself better. Astrology filled the bill. More than thirty years later, it remains the creative passion of my life as I continue to counsel, write, study, and share ideas with clients and colleagues around the world.

ACKNOWLEDGMENTS

Thanks to Paul O'Brien, our agent, our friend, and the creative genius behind Tarot.com; Gail Goldberg, the editor who always makes us sound better; Charles Nurnberg and Michael Fragnito at Sterling Publishing, for their tireless support for the project; Barbara Berger, our supervising editor, who has shepherded this book with Taurean persistence and Aquarian invention; Laura Jorstad, for her refinement of the text; and Sterling project editor Mary Hern and designer Rachel Maloney for their invaluable help. We thank Bob Wietrak and Jules Herbert at Barnes & Noble, and all of the helping hands at Sterling. Thanks for the art and ideas from Jessica Abel and the rest of the Tarot.com team. Thanks as well to 3+Co. for the original design and to Tara Gimmer for the cover photo.